Two Months
in the Camp of Big Bear

The Life and Adventures of Theresa
Gowanlock and Theresa Delaney

by Theresa Gowanlock and Theresa Delaney

with a scholarly introduction
by Sarah Carter

Canadian Plains Research Center
University of Regina
Regina, Saskatchewan
1999

Canadian Plains Research Center
University of Regina
Regina, Saskatchewan S4S 0A2
canadian.plains@uregina.ca
http://www.cprc.uregina.ca

Canadian Cataloguing in Publication Data

Gowanlock, Theresa, d. 1899.

    Two months in the camp of Big Bear: the life and adventures of Theresa Gowanlock and Theresa Delaney

    (Canadian Plains reprint series, ISSN 1208-9680 ; 4)

    Includes bibliographical references.

    ISBN 0-88977-107-3

1. Gowanlock, Theresa, d. 1899.
2. Delaney, Theresa, 1865?-1913.
3. Big Bear, 1825?-1888.
4. Cree Indians — Alberta — Captivities.
5. Frog Lake (Alta.) — History — Massacre, 1885.
6. Riel Rebellion, 1885.
I. Delaney, Theresa, 1865?-1913. II. Carter, Sarah, 1954- III. University of Regina. Canadian Plains Research Center. IV. Title. V. Series.

E85.G85 1999   971.05'4   C99-920149-2

Cover Design: Donna Achtzehner, Canadian Plains Research Center, University of Regina, Regina, Saskatchewan
Cover artwork (line drawings reproduced from the original publication of *Two Months in the Camp of Big Bear*)

Printed and bound in Canada by
Houghton Boston Printers, Saskatoon, Saskatchewan
Printed on acid-free paper

Contents

"Captured Women": A Re-examination of the Stories of Theresa Delaney and Theresa Gowanlock

Introduction to the 1999 Edition of
Two Months in the Camp of Big Bear

by Sarah Carter

Theresa Gowanlock and Theresa Delaney are not familiar names in Canadian history today, but they were among the greatest celebrities of the tumultuous events of 1885 in western Canada.[1] Visitors to the cemetery at the site of the Frog Lake settlement (in present-day Alberta) will find inscribed on a stone cairn the words "They Took Prisoners Mrs. Theresa Delaney, Mrs. Theresa Gowanlock," beneath the names of nine men, including their husbands, who were killed on April 2, 1885 by some members of Big Bear's band of Plains Cree. The settlement of Frog Lake was abandoned and destroyed in the spring of 1885, but for many years Theresa Delaney's flowers and the hedge around her garden continued to grow untended. The cellar depression of the Delaney home can still be found even though the shrubs, stunted poplars, and grasses of the parkland belt have largely reclaimed this site, and two miles away some remnants of the Gowanlock home and mill on Frog Creek are discernible. The site of Frog Lake today conveys a sense of the shattered lives of these

---

1   The ideas expressed in this "Introduction" are discussed in greater detail in Sarah Carter, *Capturing Women: The Manipulation of Cultural Imagery in Canada's Prairie West* (Montreal: McGill-Queen's University Press, 1997).

women, but visitors learn little about them beyond the words found on the stone cairn. For two months following the deaths of their husbands they were among a large group that some Plains Cree harboured while they attempted to evade confrontation and capture. During this time, and as Canada mobilized over 5,000 men to suppress what was interpreted then as a Métis and Indian "rebellion," a frenzy of media attention came to focus upon the two white women captives, or "fair daughters of Ontario." Following the defeat of the Métis at Batoche on May 12, the final task of the North-West Field Force was to pursue the Cree, and secure the safety of the hostages. Even though the Cree camp included a large number of women, men and children of diverse ancestries, the two Theresas became the focus of the campaign, which took on the appearance of a crusade to save the two white women. When they emerged at Fort Pitt early in June, telegraphs announcing the glad tidings were read in the House of Commons, and it was stated in one Ontario newspaper that:

> A thrill of pleasure will influence every Canadian man and woman on learning that Mrs. Delaney and Mrs. Gowanlock have escaped from the Indians safe and uninjured. The news will give as much genuine cause of congratulation as that of the success at Batoche.[2]

It is curious that these women, who were so central to the drama of that momentous year, are scarcely mentioned in the many histories of 1885, although their book *Two Months in the Camp of Big Bear: The Life and Adventures of Theresa Gowanlock and Theresa Delaney* is often drawn upon as an "eye-witness" account of Frog Lake.

Yet there is a great challenge involved in any attempt to restore Gowanlock and Delaney to a place in history, as it is difficult to know with any certainty what actually happened to them. From the beginning of their ordeal, and even months after, different versions of the experiences of Mrs. Gowanlock and Mrs. Delaney were presented, and their two months with the Cree came to constitute another battle-ground of 1885. These two women who emerged so suddenly from obscurity that spring found their experiences — or their imagined experiences — at the centre of a debate over the critical issues of the hour and the age: the purposes and quality of government administration of Indian affairs, and who was to blame for the events of 1885; just who deserved recognition as the heroic males of 1885; whether Aboriginal males and white women should be granted the franchise; and whether there should be a mass hanging of Aboriginal men involved in the deaths at Frog Lake and elsewhere in the North-West. At the heart of this dispute was the issue of the kind of nation Canada was to be — pluralistic or monocultural — and just what would be the expectations and roles of white women, as well as of non-white women in this new nation. Those who wished to warn against the potential dangers of a pluralistic and more egalitarian nation, and wanted to maintain and strengthen race and gender divisions and hierarchies, cast Delaney and Gowanlock as helpless and vulnerable victims of Aboriginal savagery, and it was this script that emerged triumphant. This

---

2   Canada, House of Commons, *Debates*, June 8, 1885, 2357. *Free Press* (Ottawa), June 8, 1885.

version of events was codified in November 1885 through the publication of the separate narratives of the two women in one book entitled *Two Months in the Camp of Big Bear.* In this book their suffering and privation, their helplessness and vulnerability were emphasized, although this was not quite the story that they gave early in June at Fort Pitt. While the women had clearly been through a tremendous ordeal, and an unfamiliar routine, in their first public declarations the women stressed that they had coped reasonably well under the circumstances, that they had received considerate treatment, had had plenty to eat, had not been forced to either work or walk, and were very grateful for the care and assistance of some Métis families, especially that of John and Rose Pritchard.

Two Months is reprinted here in the hope that it will encourage new ways of thinking about 1885, which is almost always presented from a purely masculine perspective. Women, both Aboriginal and non-Aboriginal, were at the centre and not the periphery of these events. Yet it is impossible to generalize about the topic of women in 1885. *Two Months* provides insight into the ways in which women of different ancestries, or "races," were categorized in the dominant society of non-Aboriginal Canada.[3] Racially specific ideas of womanhood and femininity were devised and manipulated at this time in Canada's West.[4] To be white and female in 1885, meant something quite different from being Aboriginal and female. While great sympathy was extended to the two women who were understood to have endured "the severest trials of any concerned in the whole of the rebellion in the North-West," little concern was voiced about the several Cree women who died in 1885, or Métis women and children who were left homeless and destitute.[5] During this confrontation no white women were killed or injured. It is also hoped that this reprinting will provoke careful scrutiny of texts such as *Two Months* that are often assumed to be unproblematic and accurate "eye-witness" accounts. *Two Months* does present the experiences, voices and thoughts of Gowanlock and Delaney, but it must also be appreciated that they had to contend with a variety of constraints, pressures and demands in the production of this book. The stories told in *Two Months* are selected, and they capitalized upon existing sets of images, symbols, representations and expectations. As widows they were anxious to secure government pensions and this was likely a powerful factor compelling them to place events in a certain light, to

---

3   "Race" is placed within quotation marks to indicate that it is an imagined concept, which refers to nothing that should be recognized as real. See Kwame Anthony Appiah, "Race," in Frank Lentricchia and Thomas McLaughlin (eds.), *Critical Terms for Literary Study* (Chicago: University of Chicago Press, 1990), 277.

4   On the topic of race-specific ideologies of womanhood see Vron Ware, *Beyond the Pale: White Women, Racism and History* (London: Verso, 1992); Hazel Carby, *Reconstructing Womanhood: The Emergence of the Afro-American Woman Novelist* (New York: Oxford University Press, 1987); Phylllis Palmer, *Domesticity and Dirt: Housewives and Domestic Servants in the United States, 1920-1945* (Philadelphia: Temple Press, 1989).

5   *Globe* (Toronto), July 13, 1885.

convey some impressions while suppressing others. To enhance our thinking and understanding of 1885 we need to appreciate that sources such as *Two Months* are problematic and selective, and we need to pay attention to the perspectives of many others involved in order to portray a more varied and complicated past.

Contexts: The Authors

There are multiple contexts for understanding the complex events of 1885, and many possible beginnings to histories of these events. For this publication it is perhaps most fitting to begin with the authors and their husbands. Beyond the sparse biographical detail provided in *Two Months*, little is known about the lives of these two women before and after the crisis of 1885. Theresa (née Johnson) Gowanlock was born in 1863 at Tintern in Lincoln County, Ontario, which is in the Niagara Peninsula east of Hamilton. Her parents, Martha (née Upper) and Henry Johnson, were both from pioneering families of that district and their house on the Johnson farm, where Theresa and her eight brothers and sisters were born, remained standing until very recently on the outskirts of Tintern.[6] They were a Presbyterian family. Theresa Johnson married John A. Gowanlock in October 1884. He was born in 1861 at Stratford, Ontario, and quite likely the couple met while he was visiting his sister, Elizabeth (Daisy) Huntsman of Tintern. John Gowanlock originally went west on the advice of his aunt, Dr. Jenny Kidd Trout of Toronto (the first woman licensed to practice medicine in Canada), as his health required a change in climate.[7] He worked as a farmer, speculator, surveyor and storekeeper in the Battleford district before securing a federal government contract to build and operate a grist mill on Frog Creek, with his partner Richard Laurie. In the mid-1880s the government began a program of granting bonuses to individuals who would establish mills in the Territories in the neighbourhood of Indian reserves, to address the problem of access to milling facilities.[8] The $2,000 bonus from the government secured precedence in grinding their grain for ten years for reserve farmers. The site that Gowanlock and Laurie chose on Frog Creek was right on the reserve of Chief Onepohayo. Although an Indian Affairs official asked the permission of the chief to allow the construction of the mill, it seems that ten acres was deducted from the reserve without the formal procedure of a surrender of the land according to the Indian Act, under which a majority of the male residents of a reserve had to give their

---

6 For information on Theresa Gowanlock I am grateful to Roy A.C. Johnson of Ridgeville, Ontario, family historian, for sharing his research and providing copies of the *Johnson Reporter*. I would also like to thank Margaret Comfort of Tintern for her assistance and for her article "The Village of Tintern: Tintern Bride," *Niagara Farmers' Monthly* (April 1992): 24. Art Seehagel of Tintern was also very helpful during my visit to Tintern.

7 Carlotta Hacker, *The Indomitable Lady Doctors* (Toronto: Clarke, Irwin, 1974), 39, 42.

8 Sarah Carter, *Lost Harvests: Prairie Indian Reserve Farmers and Government Policy* (Montreal: McGill-Queen's Press, 1990), 166-68.

1. Theresa Gowanlock

approval.[9] The Indian agent for the Battleford district said that this unilateral action was taken "in order to prevent any trouble or the possibility of excessive and unreasonable demands on the part of the Indians, as well as to avoid much useless talking..."[10] The federal government then agreed to lease this land to Gowanlock and Laurie. It was to this ten-acre site that John Gowanlock took his new bride late in 1884, and while the mill never operated, the map of Indian Reserve No. 121 still shows this ten-acre jog along the southern boundary. In the Battleford newspaper, the *Saskatchewan Herald*, it was noted on October 31, 1884 that while on a trip down east John Gowanlock had taken "unto himself one of Ontario's fair daughters and brought her out west to grow up with the country." They were married in Tintern, then visited Parkdale (today part of Toronto), where two of Gowanlock's brothers owned the Parkdale *Times* Newspaper, Book and Publishing Company. They immediately left for the West travelling by boat and by rail, then overland from Swift Current. Theresa Gowanlock spent six weeks in Battleford, and only arrived at Frog Creek mill in mid-December 1884. Following her brief few months in Western Canada, Theresa Gowanlock returned to her parents' home at Tintern, and died there in 1899 at age 36.[11]

Although she was often cast as a "fair daughter of Ontario" during the events of 1885, Theresa (née Fulford) Delaney was from the province of Quebec, as she was born and raised on the Aylmer Road, Hull Township, near Ottawa. Marshall and

9   George Stanley (Musunekwepan), "An Account of the Frog Lake Massacre," in Stuart Hughes (ed.), *The Frog Lake "Massacre:" Personal Perspectives on Ethnic Conflict* (Ottawa: McClelland and Stewart, 1976), 160; Keith Davidson, "Ten Acres for Theresa: A Frog Lake History Mystery," *Lloydminster Regional Times* (September 16, 1998), 9a. I am very grateful to Robert and Shirley Hendriks, Heinsburg, Alberta, for sending me the Davidson article.

10   Quoted in Davidson.

11   Theresa (Johnson) Gowanlock is buried with her parents in St. Ann's II United Churchyard. On her headstone is inscribed "Theresa M. Johnson, wife of John Gowanlock, who on April 1 1885 was taken prisoner by Big Bear during the massacre of Frog Lake, NWT and after 2 months captivity was rescued by Col. Strange, d. Sept. 12, 1899, age 36 yr, 11 m. 15d."

Bridget (née Ryan) Fulford's eldest daughter Theresa was born in 1849, and there were at least three other sisters and four brothers in this Roman Catholic family.[12] It was the lumbering business that first brought John Delaney from Nepean, Ontario, to the Aylmer Road where he worked as a foreman for a lumbering concern. But in 1879 he headed west, chosen as one of the first contingent of farm instructors to the residents of the new Indian reserves.[13] As a desperate measure to head off a food crisis in the North-West, and to assist Aboriginal farmers to learn necessary skills, a squad of farm instructors from eastern Canada was sent west in 1879. They were chosen personally from a patronage list by Prime Minister John A. Macdonald himself, so that being a loyal Conservative was a necessary and perhaps the primary qualification. They were to establish model or "home" farms, raise large quantities of food with which to feed themselves, their staff, and the Indians, and they were also to provide instruction in farming. Many of the instructors were ill-equipped for the job, as they had little experience with farming, knew nothing about conditions of life in the West, and could not speak Aboriginal languages. The program did not live up to original hopes and expectations, as the farm instructors had great difficulty establishing the most modest of farms, and they found it impossible to both farm on their own and serve as instructors to Aboriginal farmers. The plan to establish model farms was quickly shelved. Difficulties with personnel arose early on, and the program was characterized by resignations and dismissals. John Delaney, however, was one of the original farm instructors who persisted. His job was to assist Aboriginal farmers, and he was also often the person in charge of the stores and rations. As was the case with some other of the early government instructors and agents, Delaney had relationships with Cree women, and this may have been the cause of the resentment that was felt for him. In 1881 a man named Sand Fly had accused Delaney of stealing his wife, whereupon Delaney had the man charged with assault and theft. The result was a prison sentence of two and a half years, which was generally seen by all in the district as an action taken by Delaney so that he could cohabit with the prisoner's wife.[14] After three years as a farm instructor, Delaney returned to the Aylmer Road, married Theresa Fulford, and together they left for Frog Lake in August 1882. Theresa Delaney therefore, had a much longer stay at Frog Lake than Theresa Gowanlock before the upheaval of 1885. As mentioned in her narrative, Mrs. Delaney worked as "farm instructress" to the Woods Cree women, giving lessons in baking,

---

12   Thanks to Diane Aldred, Aylmer, for her research in locating the tombstone of Theresa (Fulford) Delaney in St. Paul's Roman Catholic Cemetery on the Aylmer Road. See also Anson A. Gard, *Pioneers of the Upper Ottawa and the Humours of the Valley* (Ottawa: Emerson Press, 1906), 23; Robert Fulford, "Big Bear, Frog Lake and My Aunt Theresa," *Saturday Night* (June 1976): 9-10; and Robert Fulford, "How the West Was Lost" *Saturday Night* (July 1985): 5-8.

13   Carter, *Lost Harvests*, "The Home Farm Experiment," 79-129.

14   Hugh A. Dempsey, *Big Bear: The End of Freedom* (Vancouver: Douglas and McIntyre, 1984), 117.

milking, churning, making butter, knitting and dressmaking. Theresa Delaney returned to the Aylmer Road in 1885, and there she taught school and was supported by her government pension.[15] In 1913 she died in Ottawa, where she moved shortly before her death.

Canada and the Indigenous People of the North-West

It was not until the early 1880s that non-Aboriginal women such as the two Theresas began to arrive in prairie Canada west of Manitoba, and they did not appear in large numbers until the completion of the Canadian Pacific Railway (CPR) in 1885. The railroad was the most critical component in the plan to consolidate Canada's control over the North-West, a plan pursued since before Confederation in 1867, but especially after 1869, when Canada acquired "Rupert's Land," the vast territory that the English Hudson's Bay Company (HBC) had regarded as its own since 1670. The Canadian state wished to consolidate authority over this territory against any American claims or interests, but also needed to establish control over the population of indigenous people. Mrs. Gowanlock and Mrs. Delaney were brief visitors to the ancient homeland of a great diversity of Aboriginal people who never recognized the claims of a foreign trading company to this land, or the transfer of this land to the Dominion of Canada. The people of the plains included the Assiniboine, Plains Cree, Plains Ojibway (or Saulteaux), and Blackfoot (consisting of the allied Peigan, Blood and Siksika). In the parkland transition belt and boreal forest there were also diverse people including the Woods Cree, Chipewyan, and Ojibway. Interaction with Europeans in this territory dates from the time of the early French explorers and voyageurs, and it focussed on the business of the fur trade. There were several Aboriginal groups that became active in the European fur trade, including many of the Ojibway, Cree, Assiniboine and Chipewyan. In some localities fur trade interaction was characterized by intermarriage and the emergence of people of mixed ancestry, most notably the Métis. In the early phases of the fur trade Aboriginal participants were equal to and in some respects dominant to the Europeans, but by the nineteenth century fur-trade activity had resulted in considerable damage and destruction to the environment and the economy of some Aboriginal groups, and by the last decades of that century, buffalo robe and hide trade activity helped to destroy that resource. European diseases, especially smallpox, struck with devastating consequences in epidemics of the late 1830s and late 1860s.

Aware of their dwindling resource base, and of developments in the western United States such as railways, violent encounters with the military, and the influx of settlers, Aboriginal people of western Canada entered into a series of treaties with the Canadian government during the 1870s. Canada sought treaties to acquire title to the land, as a necessary first stage to empire building, and in order to complete the

---

15   On the issue of her government pension see National Archives of Canada (NA), Record Group 10 (RG 10), Records Relating to Indian Affairs, vol. 3719, file 22649, Mrs. M.L. Walsh *et al.* to Minister of the Interior, April 14, 1915.

transcontinental railway (promised and held out as an enticement to British Columbia in 1871). This railway would encourage immigration, help to establish a prosperous agricultural economy, and strengthen industry in Central Canada. Through treaties Aboriginal people sought to enter into an equal partnership with the nation of Canada in order to secure their physical and cultural survival, to gain assistance in the transition to new economies based on agriculture and husbandry, and to establish peaceful, equitable relations.[16] These developments were not unique to Western Canada at this time, as there was a global pattern of European powers moving to consolidate control over territories in Africa, Asia, and Latin America, while in North America governments incorporated land that became part of the nation-states. As in other colonial settings this process of empire building generally involved the extension of the power of the central government, a dwindling land base for indigenous populations, the attempted domination of the colonizers over the colonized, and measures to facilitate the commercial enterprize of the colonizers. Also, as in other colonial settings, the resistance of indigenous people was met with force and, in some cases, overwhelming force.

In the Canadian West a first resistance of Aboriginal people took place in 1869-70 at the Red River Settlement (Winnipeg), when the Métis led by Louis Riel objected to the transfer of their territory to the Dominion of Canada. The Métis, by far the majority of the population at Red River, were not consulted with or informed about this transfer, and they were concerned about their land, language and religious rights. The Métis declared themselves a provisional government at a time when there was a vacuum of authority, and they entered into difficult and protracted negotiations with Canada. At Red River there was an effort to overthrow the provisional government, led by prominent men of the "Canadian Party," those who had lobbied for union with Canada. Over 40 of these men were arrested and imprisoned by the Métis, and on March 4 one of the prisoners, an Ontarian named Thomas Scott, was charged with insubordination and executed. Although this event whipped up a frenzy of hatred in Ontario, negotiations continued. In the meantime a military expedition under the command of Colonel Garnet Wolseley was dispatched west. It arrived at the end of August 1870, and while there remained no resistance to quell, its presence did amount to the military occupation of the new Canadian province. Although the Métis successfully negotiated for the provincial status for Manitoba, for land rights (1.4 million acres), and for bilingual institutions and denominational schools, most of these rights were quickly or eventually eroded. A "postage-stamp" province was created, leaving most of the territory of the North-West under firm federal control and nullifying any political power the Métis might enjoy. The Métis did not receive most of the land promised to them, while new settlers were

---

16 For general background on treaties see Treaty 7 Elders and Tribal Council, with Walter Hildebrandt, Dorothy First Rider, and Sarah Carter, *The True Spirit and Original Intent of Treaty 7* (Montreal: McGill-Queen's University Press, 1996).

Table 1 Population of the North-West in 1885				
	Whites	Métis	Indians	Total
Assiniboia	16,574	1,017	4,492	22,083
Saskatchewan	4,486*		6,260	10,746
Alberta	4,878	1,254	9,418	15,533
Total	25,938	2,254*	20,170	48,362

*The Saskatchewan figure includes whites and Métis.
Source: P.B. Waite, *Canada 1874-1896: Arduous Destiny* (Toronto: McClelland and Stewart, 1971), 149.

given every encouragement.[17] Bilingual and denominational school rights were also eroded. Large numbers of the Red River Métis moved further west in the 1870s, settling at locations such as Batoche and St. Laurent on the South Saskatchewan River.

By 1884 another crisis in colonial authority was brewing in the North-West, where in some districts the Aboriginal population greatly outnumbered the Euro-Canadians (see Table 1). Since the mid-1870s the Métis of the South Saskatchewan settlements expressed concern that their land rights be recognized. As surveys proceeded and new settlers began to surround them, the Métis remained without recognized title to their land. Meanwhile, the CPR and the HBC were being granted enormous parcels of land in what was regarded as the fertile belt, while the great majority of First Nations were granted reserves. A host of non-Aboriginal residents of Western Canada warned the federal government that the Métis land question had to be dealt with as there could be a challenge to the peace and prosperity of the West, and there was considerable support and sympathy for the Métis. Many of the recent non-Aboriginal arrivals also had grievances directed at the federal government. These warnings were not heeded, however, and the federal government took no action to make satisfactory arrangements with the Métis. In 1884 a delegation of Saskatchewan Métis persuaded Louis Riel, then living in Montana, to return with them and assist in their campaign for rights. Riel held public meetings with Métis and the new settlers, and he wrote a comprehensive petition with clauses concerning Métis land rights and territorial self-government. Frustrated by the lack of federal action, the Métis began to talk of the use of force, and the support of other settlers fell away. They seized arms and ammunition and on March 19 elected a provisional government. Several days later, Major General Frederick Middleton, commanding the Canadian military, received orders to put the militia onto alert. The first confrontation

---

17 See D.N. Sprague, *Canada and the Métis, 1869-1885* (Waterloo: Wilfrid Laurier University Press, 1988).

2. *Big Bear*

broke out at Duck Lake when the Métis encountered a government force commanded by the North-West Mounted Police (NWMP). The strategy of the North-West Field Force was to proceed north in three columns from three points along the CPR. The column commanded by Middleton headed from Qu'Appelle station (Troy) toward Batoche, while Lieutenant Colonel William Otter led his men from Swift Current to Battleford, where the non-Aboriginal residents had barricaded themselves in the NWMP post. Major General Thomas Bland Strange took his column from Calgary toward Edmonton, and it was primarily his men that were engaged in the pursuit of Big Bear's camp.

Frog Lake

Frog Lake was in the parkland or transition belt that divides the open grasslands from the forested northern regions of Western Canada. It had long been the home of the Woods Cree who had an economy that took advantage of the resources of both the plains and the parkland. In 1879 two reserves were surveyed on Frog Lake — that of Chief Onepohayo and that of Chief Pus-kee-ah-kee-he-win. Onepohayo was head chief of the Woods Cree during the resistance of 1885, having succeeded his father Chaschakiskwis, who had taken Treaty 6 in 1876 on behalf of the Woods Cree of Frog Lake. He was quoted as saying in 1876 that "I am truly glad that the Queen has made a new country for me. I am glad that all my friends and children will not be in want of food hereafter."[18] This was not to be the case, however; the early years of reserve life were times of great want as the buffalo had been exterminated, and farming on the reserves progressed slowly. Throughout the North-West there was disappointment at the failure of the federal government to live up to promises made at treaty time that there would be assistance in providing the necessities to establish an agricultural economy.[19] Implements and livestock promised in the treaty were inadequate and inferior, there were problems with the quality and distribution of seed grain, and it was impossible for people to congregate in order to seed and to attend crops when there was nothing to live on. All

---

18   Alexander Morris, *The Treaties of Canada with the Indians of Manitoba and the North-West Territories* (1880; Toronto: Coles Publishing, 1971), 239.

19   Carter, *Lost Harvests*, chapter 2, "The 'Queen's Bounty': Government Response to Indian Agitation for Agricultural Assistance," 50-78.

3. *Thomas Quinn*

of these factors made it necessary for some band members to remain very mobile in searching for resources off the reserves. There were rations for reserve residents, but these were given out sparingly, in return for assigned work, and rations were at times curtailed altogether. A new policy of financial entrenchment was in place from late in 1883, when policymakers decided that rations should be issued to the aged only, and that some groups did not require rations at all. In 1884 there were reports that reserve residents throughout the North-West were very down-cast, in poor health, and worried that they were going to starve. People did not have adequate shelter, clothing or footwear.

In the fall of 1884 the resources of the Frog Lake district were strained even further by the arrival of Big Bear and his Plains Cree followers who numbered just over 500, almost equalling the combined population of the reserves at Frog Lake, Onion Lake and Long Lake. Big Bear was a chief of the Fort Pitt district who was renowned for his visions, medicine and political skill. He had refused to take Treaty 6 and from 1876 he pursued a strategy aimed at securing better treaty terms, and at preserving the autonomy and integrity of the Cree.[20] Well before the events of 1885 and the publication of *Two Months in the Camp of Big Bear*, the chief was well-known throughout non-Aboriginal Canada, having gained a reputation as an obstreperous troublemaker. Big Bear and his followers spent several years of severe hardship, first in the northern plains of the United States, and then in the vicinity of Fort Walsh in the Cypress Hills. Big Bear's authority and stature among his own people eroded during these years, as his followers were not eligible for any of the rations and supplies that were given to treaty people. In 1882, faced with the anger and impatience of his people, Big Bear accepted the treaty, but as his last negotiating point he delayed selecting a reserve site for his band. This, too, generated anger and discontent among his followers. A reserve site was under negotiation in the district of Frog Lake in the fall of 1884, but Big Bear delayed moving there when his requests for extra rations were turned down. Permission was sought from Onepohayo to allow Big Bear to camp

---

20 See Dempsey, *Big Bear*, and John L. Tobias, "Canada's Subjugation of the Plains Cree, 1879-1885," *Canadian Historical Review* 64, no. 4 (1983): 519-48.

on his reserve and this is where they spent the winter of 1884-85 which was one of great hardship. The Frog Lake district was almost entirely devoid of game that year, and it was an extremely cold winter with deep snow. Yet while confidence in Big Bear's leadership was diminishing among some of his followers, the chief's broader campaign to consolidate the Cree appeared to be gaining momentum by 1884, as he was twice able to convene councils of important Cree leaders to discuss treaty violations. This gathering momentum was alarming to government officials, who were pursuing a policy of dispersing and weakening the Cree.

A settlement of Métis and non-Aboriginal people emerged at Frog Lake in the early 1880s when John Delaney constructed a house, warehouse and shed. By 1885 the village consisted of an HBC post, the buildings of the Indian agency, a Roman Catholic mission, a store operated by George Dill, and a six-man NWMP detachment. Thomas Quinn was the Indian subagent at Frog Lake. He was of part Dakota ancestry, and he was married to a Cree woman named Owl Sitting (also known as Jane Quinn after her marriage). Just before the violent outbreak of April 2, and for reasons that remain obscure, the NWMP evacuated Frog Lake and went to Fort Pitt. One explanation is that Quinn sent them away, as he was confident that he could command the respect of his charges, and he was concerned that the NWMP could become a target following events at Duck Lake.[21] Among the residents of Frog Lake who were later to be part of Big Bear's camp along with Mrs. Gowanlock and Mrs. Delaney were John Pritchard, his wife Rose (Delorme) and their eight children. Pritchard, a Métis, was the interpreter for the government Indian agency. Interpreters were vital at these agencies as most employees, such as John Delaney, were unable to speak the languages of the people they worked among. Pritchard spoke English and French, as well as Cree and several other Aboriginal languages. He had spent some years studying for the ministry of the Anglican church, and although he did not follow this calling he remained devoutly religious.[22]

"April is the cruellest month," wrote T.S. Eliot, and he could certainly have been describing the parkland belt of Western Canada.[23] April 1885 was particularly cruel because it had been a winter of great hardship and there few signs that winter was over. Yet the earliest non-Aboriginal accounts of the events at Frog Lake stressed that there were no indications of unrest or difficulties in the entire district; it was a happy, placid settlement where a benevolent little group laboured long and zealously to

---

21 Desmond Morton, *The Last War Drum: The North West Campaign of 1885* (Toronto: A.M. Hakkert, 1972), 23. For further context and background please see Walter Hildebrandt, *Views from Fort Battleford: Constructed Visions of an Anglo-Canadian West* (Regina: Canadian Plains Research Center, 1994), and Walter Hildebrandt, *The Battle of Batoche: British Small Warfare and the Entrenched Metis* (Ottawa: Environment Canada, 1985).

22 C.D. Denney, "In Memory of Mary Rose (Pritchard) Sayers: The Last Witness," *Saskatchewan History* 24, no. 2 (Spring 1971): 63, 67.

23 T.S. Eliot, *The Waste Land and Other Poems* (London: Faber and Faber, 1985), 27.

4. Graves of the victims of Frog Lake

better the lives of their Indian neighbours.[24] The outbreak of violence was unpredictable, and was due to the fierce, savage temperament of Aboriginal people. In these non-Aboriginal accounts blame was also laid on the nefarious influence of Riel, on the sinister Métis of the Frog Lake settlement, on the notorious Big Bear and his malign influence, and on the perfidy and collusion of the HBC.

Accounts from the perspectives of Aboriginal people stressed the frustrations with government policy and with individual employees, as well as the conditions of poverty and starvation in the district and the multiple tensions that had built up.[25] Mary Dion

24 See, for example, G.M. Adam, *From Savagery to Civilization: The Canadian North-West, Its History and Its Troubles* (Toronto: Rose Publishing, 1885), 301-16. Other accounts such as William B. Cameron's *Blood Red the Sun*, are contained in Hughes, *The Frog Lake "Massacre."*

25 Norma Sluman and Jean Goodwill, *John Tootoosis: A Biography of a Cree Leader* (Ottawa: Golden Dog Press, 1982). See also George Stanley (Musunekwepan) in Hughes, *The Frog Lake Massacre*; Isabelle Little Bear, "My Own Story: Isabelle Little Bear, One of the Last Remaining Links with the Riel Rebellion," in Mary Bennett (ed.), *Reflections: A History of*

told her grandson, author Joe Dion, about many instances of the casual cruelty of the white people at Frog Lake, their disdain and contempt, and their merriment at the sight of human misery.[26] That was a winter of great hardship, as there was never enough food, and in order to receive the meagre rations, debilitating work had to be performed in subzero temperatures, and in threadbare clothing.

On the morning of April 2, and under the leadership not of Big Bear, but of Wandering Spirit, and Ayimasis, one of Big Bear's sons, some of the Plains Cree began to remove goods from the stores at Frog Lake, and to round up prisoners, including Quinn, the Gowanlocks, the Delaneys and the Pritchards. Big Bear had been away hunting for over two weeks, and had just returned on April 1. They were ordered to move with the Cree to a new camp but Quinn adamantly refused, and he was shot by Wandering Spirit. In short order, Charles Gouin (a Métis carpenter employed by the Indian agency), John Delaney, John Gowanlock, Father Adelarde Fafard, Father Félix Marchand (visiting from Onion Lake), John Williscraft (Fafard's lay assistance), George Dill, and William Gilchrist (Gowanlock's clerk) all met the same fate.

With the Cree

The two widowed women were quickly pulled from their husbands, but from this point on it becomes a challenge to discern precisely what happened to them, as competing and conflicting versions were presented. In 1885 and for years afterward, the question of just who "saved" the white women from death or the "fate worse than death," was hotly contested, with many trying to take or assign credit, while discrediting others who tried to do so. According to Musunekwepan, the seventeen-year-old son of Chief Onepohayo, the terrified and distraught women were first taken to the tipi of his father, who assured them that they would not be harmed, while his mother gave them water.[27] According to this source Big Bear set aside a tent for the women and ordered John Pritchard and another Métis to watch over them. At a meeting of Woods and Plains Cree, Chiefs Onepohayo and Big Bear warned others of the dangers that might be incurred if the prisoners were harmed, and it was decided that a close guard of five men, including Pritchard, would be kept over the women. Other Aboriginal accounts credit the persuasive skills of the Woods Cree for arranging that

---

Elk Point and District (Winnipeg: Inter-Collegiate Press, 1977), 197-202; and the accounts contained in *Land of Red and White* (Heinsburg: Frog Lake Community Club, 1977) and *Fort Pitt Unfolding, 1829-1925* (Frenchman Butte: Fort Pitt Historical Society, 1985). Recent histories that attempt to bring together multiple perspectives are Bob Beal and Rod Macleod, *Prairie Fire: The 1885 North-West Rebellion* (Edmonton: Hurtig Publishers, 1984), 179-204; Blair Stonechild and Bill Waiser, *Loyal Till Death: Indians and the North-West Rebellion* (Calgary: Fifth House Publishers, 1997), 106-25.

26 Joe Dion, *My Tribe the Crees* (Calgary: Glenbow-Alberta Institute, 1979), 91-92.

27 Stanley, (Musunekwepan), "An Account of the Frog Lake Massacre," in Hughes, *The Frog Lake "Massacre,"* 164-65.

the women be placed in safe custody.[28] In W.B. Cameron's first statements to the press he also credited the Woods Cree with the strategy that saved the white women, but in his account published in later years, *Blood Red the Sun*, Cameron accords no credit to any Cree, and gave a lengthy description of how Pritchard and another Métis, Adolphus Nolin, had cleverly outwitted the Plains Cree and purchased Mrs. Delaney from her Cree captors.[29] Cameron wrote that a Métis by the name of Pierre Blondin played a role in securing the safety of Mrs. Gowanlock, but Cameron condemned Blondin's subsequent conduct. In his later years Cameron said that he could have escaped from the Cree camp much earlier than he did, but did not want to leave the two women behind, suggesting that he too shared a measure of responsibility for their safety.[30] In his memoirs of events Métis Louis Goulet claimed that he was responsible for persuading Blondin to assist him in the purchase of Mrs. Gowanlock, and that it was he (Goulet) who then left her in the care of Pritchard.[31] As will be discussed later in greater detail, when Mrs. Gowanlock and Mrs. Delaney first emerged from their ordeal, they credited Pritchard, Nolin, and Blondin for their safety, but this is altered to some extent in the written account. Blondin appears as a central villain of the story — a man aware of sinister plans for Frog Lake, interested in acquiring Mrs. Gowanlock only for his own nefarious purposes, and in the habit of parading before her wearing her dead husband's clothing. Although it is not clear just how it was arranged, it is certain that for the next two months the women were billeted with the Pritchard family.

At this point Mrs. Delaney and Mrs. Gowanlock were far from the only reluctant adjuncts in the camp of Big Bear, and their numbers were to be greatly augmented over the next weeks. They included a mixture of the many diverse peoples of the North-West. Mrs. Quinn, another widow of the events of Frog Lake, and her daughter, were in the camp. William B. Cameron, a young HBC clerk, survived that day (and in 1925 he was shocked and disappointed that his name did not appear on the cairn at Frog Lake as one of those also taken prisoner). Credit for saving Cameron's life has been generally attributed to Catherine Simpson, the wife of James Simpson, who ran the HBC store at Frog Lake. She and Mrs. John Horse hastily disguised Cameron by wrapping him in a red shawl, and concealed him until the shooting was over. James Simpson was a son of Sir George Simpson and one of his "country-born" wives, and Catherine was reported in several accounts to have been a

---

28 See Dion, *My Tribe the Crees*, and Jimmy Chief's recollections in *Fort Pitt History Unfolding*, 101.

29 William B. Cameron, *Blood Red the Sun* (1926; Vancouver: The Wrigley Printing Company Ltd., 1950), chapter 10, "The Rescue of the White Women," 67-71.

30 Reg Taylor, "Fort Pitt Soon Captured..." in Jessie DeGear Papers, Glenbow Archives, scrapbook no. 8, p. 32.

31 Guillaume Charette, *Vanishing Spaces: Memoirs of a Prairie Métis* (Winnipeg: Editions Boîs-Brulés, 1976), 158-59.

sister of Gabriel Dumont. The Simpson family, which included her grown-up sons Louis and Benjamin Patenaude (who were treaty Indians), absorbed into the Plains Cree camp.[32] James Simpson was away at Fort Pitt that day, but on his return drove to the camp, and his horses were confiscated. One list of those taken prisoner at Frog Lake includes Peter St. Luke and his family of five.[33] Edward François Dufresne, Indian Department cook, was another white survivor of that day, and his wife Marguerite Mondion was also brought into the camp. Dufresne was from Quebec and had worked for the HBC for over fifty years.[34] Louis Goulet, Adolphus Nolin, André Nault, Pierre Blondin, and other Métis were also part of the Plains Cree camp. On April 3 a group of Cree brought two other white men to the camp: John Fitzpatrick, farm instructor for the Chipewyans at Cold Lake, and Henry R. Halpin, HBC clerk at the same place. Big Bear had sent his son-in-law, Lone Man, to retrieve these men, as he was concerned about their safety.[35] A man by the name of John Perry, who arrived at Frog Lake on April 3 to attend Good Friday services, immediately sought the safety of John Pritchard and another Métis, and he remained with Big Bear's camp for the next few months. The Woods Cree were also among the "unhappy campers," although the non-Aboriginal public found this impossible to believe, just as it was questioned whether the Métis could possibly also be prisoners. Musunekwepan recalled that when he located his parents' tipi at the Plains Cree camp he saw that the Holy Stem was placed just outside: "It was in the centre. They had put it there purposely to show that we were captured."[36]

These numbers were greatly augmented following the fall of Fort Pitt in mid-April. The HBC's Fort Pitt was a small huddle of buildings on the North Saskatchewan under the supervison of a Scotsman, Chief Trader W.J. McLean. He had served twenty years with the company at various locations and was posted to Fort Pitt in 1884. His wife Helen was born at Fort Dunvegan and was partly of Aboriginal ancestry. There were eight McLean children, and in the spring of 1885 Helen McLean was expecting another child. The three eldest McLean sisters — Amelia, Eliza and Kitty — were well educated, having attended school at Red River, but they could also ride, shoot, and were fluent in Cree and Saulteaux. There were other employees of the HBC resident at the Fort, all of whom found themselves with the Plains Cree camp, including clerk Stanley Simpson, servant Malcolm McDonald, and cook Robert Hodson. Hodson, an Englishman, had been a hangman but as this was not steady work he had served with the HBC for a number of years; Hodson executed the eight

---

32 Doug Light, *Footprints in the Dust* (North Battleford: Turner-Warwick Publications, 1987), 208.

33 Saskatchewan Archives Board (SAB), Campbell Innes Papers, Box 2, file 9, "History of the Saskatchewan Uprising," 45.

34 Light, *Footprints in the Dust*, 208.

35 Stonechild and Waiser, *Loyal Till Death*, 119.

36 Stanley (Musunekwepan), in Hughes, *The Frog Lake "Massacre,"* 164.

condemned men at Battleford in November 1885 and the following year he was appointed public hangman for the Dominion of Canada.[37] Another HBC employee at Fort Pitt was servant Alfred (Rabaska) Schmidt with his family of six.

The population of Fort Pitt had dramatically increased in the early weeks of April as people from the surrounding districts sought protection there, some with the assistance of Aboriginal associates. There were twenty-three NWMP stationed at the fort under the command of Francis Dickens (the son of the famous novelist Charles Dickens). These included the police who had evacuated Frog Lake. Other recent arrivals included an English couple, Reverend Charles and Mrs. Quinney. He was the Church of England missionary at Onion Lake, and they had been escorted to Fort Pitt on the advice of Woods Cree Chief Seekaskootch and councillors, who wished to ensure their safety.[38] Mrs. Quinney was in the later stages of pregnancy in the spring of 1885, and gave birth to a boy on June 21 at Battleford.[39] The Onion Lake agency farm instructor, George Mann, his wife Sarah (both originally from Bowmanville, Ontario), and their three children also took refuge at Fort Pitt. They, too, had been warned of danger and were escorted to Fort Pitt by people of the Onion Lake reserve who feared for their safety.[40]

The people of Fort Pitt could have evacuated for Battleford. Chief Seekaskootch initially urged them to construct rafts and leave by the river, but they opted to stay. Steps were taken to barricade the fort, and sentries were posted in front of the five buildings, with the eldest McLean sisters taking their turn at sentry duty. This routine lasted almost two weeks, when on April 14 a Plains Cree party from Frog Lake, including Big Bear, assembled on a ridge overlooking Fort Pitt. Through a messenger they asked to speak to McLean, who met with them for lengthy talks. McLean was on friendly terms with these people and believed that he did not have to fear for himself or his family. The talks lasted into a second day but a violent enounter broke out when the Cree thought themselves to be under attack. In statements made later McLean never hesitated to lay the blame for this on the poor judgement of Inspector Dickens, who, the day before, had sent out two NWMP and one civilian to gather information on the whereabouts of Aboriginal groups.[41] Their sudden appearance led the Cree to believe that they were under attack. One NWMP was killed (Constable David Cowan), another wounded (Constable Clarence Loasby), while the civilian (Thomas Quinn, nephew of Thomas Quinn) escaped briefly and was caught later that day. Three Cree were also killed during this confrontation. Following this event, all of the inhabitants of Fort Pitt, except for the NWMP, agreed to evacuate the fort, and become part of

---

37 Light, *Footprints in the Dust*, 534.

38 *Fort Pitt History Unfolding*, 42.

39 Light, *Footprints in the Dust*, 501.

40 *Fort Pitt History Unfolding*, 42.

41 W.J. McLean, "Tragic Events at Frog Lake and Fort Pitt During the North West Rebellion," in Hughes, *The Frog Lake "Massacre,"* 245-49.

Big Bear's camp. Under cover of darkness the NWMP escaped on a scow down the river to Battleford. Just how and why all of this occurred, and in the way it did, is another of the controversial questions of 1885. Dickens was criticized by some for this inglorious retreat, but in his memoirs McLean stressed that men such as Wandering Spirit despised the police, and they would not otherwise have survived. McLean was also criticized for not escaping, for not "holding the fort," and for giving himself, his family and others up to Big Bear. McLean and the other forty-four inhabitants of the fort did decide to opt for the protection of Big Bear, and also of the Woods Cree. The Quinneys, for example, sought the advice of Chief Seekaskootch, who assured them that they would be well cared for. Everyone was "billeted" with Woods or Plains Cree families, according to McLean. Amelia and Kitty McLean had shown their bravery but also their confidence in their friendship with the Cree when they walked into the camp unescorted just after the confrontation, and while their mother and sister tended to Loasby's wounds. They wanted to see if their father was safe, and Amelia declared they were not afraid: "We have lived together as brothers and sisters for many years. We speak the same language. Why should we be afraid of you?"[42] The people of Fort Pitt gathered their belongings and left for Big Bear's camp. It was an intensely cold night and soon developed into a blinding snowstorm. As the McLeans neared the camp, some of the Cree came out to greet them and, according to Elizabeth McLean, showed her mother the greatest respect:

> They gave a hand in setting up the tent which she had sent out ahead of her, and rendered very useful little services in view of the impending snowstorm, which came upon us during the night as expected.[43]

The absorption of the people of Fort Pitt into the camp, and that of other people gathered from the surrounding countryside, suggests that Big Bear and the Woods Cree leaders saw this as essential in order to protect those whose lives might be in danger. The great number of the "captives" or "prisoners" had opted for the protection of the Cree camp, upon the advice of Aboriginal friends or leaders. This was difficult for the non-Aboriginal public in the world beyond to comprehend. This large group began to move toward Frog Lake on April 17 to join up with those left at that camp, which included most of the Woods and Plains Cree women and children, and others such as Mrs. Gowanlock and Mrs. Delaney. Two days later the Fort Pitt group arrived at Frog Lake, and remained there for the next two weeks. During this time the numbers in this camp grew further, as a group of Saulteaux, travelling to visit relatives in Edmonton, were detained by the Plains Cree.[44] The Chipewyan from Cold Lake voluntarily joined the group, accompanied by their priest, the Reverent Laurent Legoff, who held divine services in the camp.[45] The entire encampment was so large

---

42 Duncan McLean with Eric Wells, published as "The Last Hostage," in Harold Fryer (ed.), *Frog Lake Massacre* (Surrey, BC: Frontier Books, 1984), 81-82.

43 Elizabeth McLean, "The Siege of Fort Pitt," *Beaver* (December 1946): 22.

44 Elizabeth McLean, "Prisoners of the Indians," *Beaver* (June 1947): 15.

that during the two (and for some people closer to three) months certain people rarely saw each other. Mrs. Gowanlock and Mrs. Delaney, for example, rarely saw the McLeans.

On May 1 this camp began to move in an easterly direction. They did not go far, and remained for some weeks in the vicinity of Frenchman Butte. Although some of the Plains Cree favoured trying to join up with Chief Poundmaker at Cut Knife Hill, or heading toward Batoche, both of these options were discarded, after a scout informed them that Battleford was teeming with soldiers and horses.[46] Big Bear maintained a neutral stance. During all of April and most of May, there was no evidence of any soldiers in pursuit. Middleton and Otter were engaged elsewhere, and Strange's column took weeks to take shape, as he had difficulties finding staff officers, and supplies such as rifles, ammunition and saddlery.[47] Strange's column did not set out from Calgary until April 20, and by May 1 had only reached Edmonton. From there Strange built a "navy" of "leaky makeshift barges" to take half his troops along the North Saskatchewan, while the other half marched, but they did not leave Edmonton until the middle of May.

The Cree and other assorted campers experienced a fairly monotonous routine. An out-of-the-ordinary event that took place in the early weeks of May was the murder of an old woman in the camp, who had become very ill, then delirious, and according to Cree belief, was in danger of becoming a cannibal, or *windigo*. As Amelia McLean Paget explained in a book she wrote entitled *The People of the Plains*, the people had no asylums or any means of isolating people who were mentally ill, "so that any person showing marked signs of insanity was dispatched…"[48] The Cree were in the midst of holding a Thirst Dance near Frenchman Butte when they learned that soldiers were approaching. In preparation for confrontation, rifle pits were dug at carefully chosen positions, and in the scrubby woods behind these rifle pits earthworks were dug for the protection of women, children and the elderly. (The depressions left from these may still be seen at Frenchman Butte National Historic Site.) The confrontation was only a minor skirmish, but was elevated to the title "Battle of Frenchman's Butte" when medals were issued for the campaign. On the morning of May 28, the soldiers opened fire, but did not attempt a direct assault, as they found the Cree position to be too strong. A sharp fire was maintained for about three hours, but then, fearing that the Cree were going to encircle them, and with three men wounded, Strange decided to retreat to Fort Pitt. The Cree did not pursue the retreating soldiers, but abandoned this site with their entourage, and headed in a northerly direction, toward Loon Lake.

---

45 See Anonymous, "Fr. Laurent Legoff O.M.I. During the Rebellion," in Hughes, *The Frog Lake "Massacre,"* 298-302.

46 W.J. McLean, in Hughes, ed., *The Frog Lake "Massacre,"* 257.

47 Morton, *The Last War Drum,* chapter 7, "Capturing Big Bear," 127-44.

48 Amelia M. Paget, *People of the Plains,* (Toronto: William Briggs, 1909), 56-57.

Imagined Experiences of Mrs. Gowanlock and Mrs. Delaney

During April and May the attention of the non-Aboriginal public became increasingly fixated on the fate, and especially the imagined fates, of the widowed white women of Frog Lake. From the time that news of the events at Frog Lake became known to the wider public, hideous tales of their deaths and/or mistreatment circulated. The earliest of the reports included Mrs. Gowanlock among the dead. She was described as having pinioned the arms of the man who had killed her husband as he aimed his rifle at another; the man was said to have shaken her off and fired, killing her instantly.[49] By mid-April the sad fate of the Gowanlocks was lamented across the nation, although there was now greater concern for the fate of Mrs. Delaney. In the Charlottetown *Daily Patriot* on April 14, the story of the Gowanlocks was described as:

> the most touching of all ... their death now at the hands of the Indians is unspeakably sad, but not so horrible probably, as the fate of Mrs. Delaney, wife of the murdered farm instructor, who was carried off a prisoner by the blood-thirsty fiends.

It was the NWMP that escaped from Fort Pitt who first verified that both Mrs. Gowanlock and Mrs. Delaney were alive and were billeted with Métis in the Cree camp, and that this had been learned from Chief Seekaskootch. But during May rumours that they were being treated horribly flourished in the media and among the military. Some newspapers, generally those that supported the Conservative administration, were not as quick to print these rumours. In the *Toronto Daily Mail* it was insisted that there was little fear that the women would be ill treated, since "outrages [*sic*] of this sort has never been, and is not now, an Indian habit."[50] Other papers, however, conveyed an image of brutal treatment given the hapless brides, or "Ontario's fair daughters," and by the later weeks of May these horrifying tales abounded, inflaming public opinion, and galvanizing the troops. The attention of the public was trained on the captive white women by the end of May when the last task of the field force was to capture Big Bear and the perpetrators of the Frog Lake murders. There was criticism, in some quarters, of Strange's delay and hints at his incompetence. The *Toronto Morning News* claimed that it was "scandalous apathy" and a discredit to humanity that so little was being done to release the captives from their "inhuman custodians." This would surely encourage similar atrocities on defenceless women, stated the *News*. The field force must "impress upon Indians that the honour of a white woman is sacred, and that outrage and murder will be promptly avenged, no matter at what cost."[51]

By the end of May it was widely reported in newspapers, and circulated throughout the field force that Mrs. Delaney had died, after being repeatedly "outraged."[52] There were various reports about Mrs. Gowanlock, that her body had

---

49   *Toronto Daily Mail,* April 14, 1885.

50   Ibid., April 23, 1885.

51   *Toronto Morning News,* May 25, 1885.

been found dumped in a well, and that she had been made the wife of an Indian.[53] The fate of the McLean sisters did not receive as much coverage, but there were rumours that they too had "suffered the final outrage." A surgeon with the Alberta Field Force wrote some years later that the "revolting" stories of the fate of the women wound the "whole force up to a pitch of fury." He added, "Had Big Bear and his band fallen into our hands while these reports were credited, I do not think man, woman, or child would have been spared."[54] From other quarters there were calls for a war of extermination against Big Bear's band. After describing how Mrs. Delaney purportedly met her end, the editor of the *Macleod Gazette* asked, "Will you blame us if we kill men, women and children of such an outfit?" and replied, "No but we will never forgive you if you don't."[55]

Rumours of the supposed fate of the white women were used to justify extremely harsh measures against the "enemy" but they also served other purposes. Those who wished to condemn government administration seized upon the tales of the women's mistreatment and death. It was suggested in the *Moosomin Courier* that the government should get an

> illuminated copy of the account of Mrs. Delaney and Mrs. Gowanlock's treatment at the hands of Big Bear's band, nicely framed and hung conspicuously in the Legislative Hall in memoriam of the hellish effects of their 'Dishwater Administration' in the North-West Territories.[56]

Mrs. Gowanlock and Mrs. Delaney also found themselves part of a debate about the Macdonald government's 1885 Electoral Franchise Act. As initially introduced on March 19, 1885, the act provided that Indian males as well as white widows and unmarried women who met the necessary qualifications would be granted the franchise. The bill was the subject of heated debate in the House of Commons and the press throughout the course of the Resistance of 1885, and it was suggested at the time and since that this was a diversionary tactic devised by Macdonald to draw attention away from the events in the West.[57] The bill also helped the prime minister to appear enlightened on Indian affairs at a time when his policy was under attack.

---

52   These rumours may have begun with a letter written by Captain and Quarter-Master R. LaTouche Tupper of the 92nd Winnipeg Light Infantry to a friend in Minnedosa, which appeared in the *Minnedosa Tribune*, May 22, 1885. See also Charles R. Daoust, *Cent-vingt jours de service actif: Recit historique très complet de la campagne du 65eme au Nord-Ouest* (1886; English translation by Roberta Cummings, Wetaskiwin: City of Wetaskiwin, 1982), 58.

53   *Free Press* (Ottawa), May 29, 1885.

54   John P. Pennefather, "Thirteen Years on the Prairies," in Harold Fryer, *Frog Lake Massacre*, 61, 71.

55   *Macleod Gazette*, June 6, 1885.

56   Quoted in ibid.

57   Sprague, *Canada and the Métis*, 176. See also Richard H. Bartlett, "Citizens Minus: Indians and the Right to Vote," *Saskatchewan Law Review* 44 (1979-80): 163-94.

Although the extension of the franchise to widows and unmarried women was soon dropped from the bill, the question of the "Indian vote" remained before the House during the weeks of military engagement in the West. In the press much scorn was heaped on the notion that the franchise would be granted to those who had been "butchering women and children" (events which did not happen).[58] Sensational fabrications about the fate of Theresa Delaney were used as ammunition against the franchise bill. Readers of the Ottawa *Free Press* were warned that the bill

> would confer the ballot upon the wretches who dishonoured Mrs. Delaney, till her death mercifully relieved her of the sense of the ignominy to which she had been compulsorily and brutally subjected.[59]

The issues of woman suffrage and the Indian franchise were often linked. This same editorial was critical of a bill that would give the vote to the "savage" who had "violated the unfortunate woman until she died, but refuse it to the intellegent women of Canada, who might use their ballots to avenge their sister's wrongs." The act that was eventually passed gave the federal vote only to all adult male Indians in Eastern Canada who met the necessry property qualifications, with Western Canadian Indians excluded entirely. The power of white males of the middle-class to claim exclusive rights to full citizenship was upheld and sustained in this case by drawing upon images of the "savages" at the margins of the new nation, and upon images of weak and vulnerable white womanhood.

The frenzy over Mrs. Gowanlock and Mrs. Delaney, and in particular the insistence that they had been subjected to rape or "outrage," has parallels in other colonial settings at times of crisis in colonial authority. Terrifying stories of brutalities to white women took hold of the colonial imagination during the Indian Rebellion in India in 1857, and the Jamaican "revolt" of 1865, bearing no resemblance to the actual level of rape or assault.[60] In the case of the Great Mutiny, it has been argued that this crisis in British authority was managed and British strategies of counter-insurgency introduced through the circulation of stories about the violation of English women.[61] The threat of violence against white women was a rationale for securing greater control, for suppressing indigenous people, and clarifying boundaries between colonizers and colonized. Even when these stories of attacks on white women were shown to be illusory, they remained fixed in memory, and on canvas and ink. Some of the tales that circulated about Mrs. Gowanlock and Mrs.

---

58 *London Advertiser*, May 5, 1885.

59 *Free Press* (Ottawa), May 22, 1885.

60 Jenny Sharpe, "The Unspeakable Limits of Rape: Colonial Violence and Counter-Insurgency," *Genders* 10 (Spring 1991); Jenny Sharpe, *Allegories of Empire: The Figure of Woman in the Colonial Text* (Minneapolis: University of Minnesota Press, 1993); Norman Etherington, "Natal's Black Rape Scare of the 1870s," *Journal of Southern African Studies* 15, no. 1 (1988).

61 See Sharpe, "Unspeakable Limits," and *Allegories of Empire.*

Delaney drew upon the stockpile of horrors from the British colonial world. Similarly the idea that they had been subjected to brutal treatment proved resilient, even after they emerged safely from their ordeal to declare that the rumours were not true. Another feature that 1885 shared with other colonial crises was that the image projected of indigenous women during the months of conflict was of their horrible brutality.[62] All of these were absolute fabrications but they served to further inflame non-Aboriginal public opinion.

Safe and Unharmed

By the end of their two months with the Cree the idea predominated that two vulnerable and helpless white women had been cruelly mistreated by their captors, and had likely died as a result. It came as a great relief, as well as a surprise, to learn early in June that they were alive and well. The women arrived at Fort Pitt on June 5 along with forty-three Métis men, women and children, including the Pritchards. This group had taken leave of the Cree camp some days after the confrontation at Frenchman Butte. Under cover of heavy fog one morning they had fallen to the rear and then struck off to the east. It is likely that they were allowed to leave, and that this was not strictly an escape. For three days they had travelled in different directions through the bush until they were located by a party of ten of General Strange's scouts led by William McKay and Peter Ballendine, both Métis. The Quinneys and others, including W.B. Cameron, had escaped some days earlier, with the assistance of Woods Cree. On June 17 a group that included the Manns and the McLeans were allowed to leave the Cree camp.

There were several correspondents on the scene at Fort Pitt, and in their initial statements Mrs. Gowanlock and Mrs. Delaney announced that they had been treated well, had had plenty to eat, and had been subjected to no cruelties or "indignities."[63] There were occasions when the menacing behaviour of certain individuals made them fear for their lives and their "virtue," and both had suffered mental anxiety, but they had been well protected, and had met with little suffering. They had cooked and laundered, but had not been forced to do these tasks; they had done them of their own accord because it had given them some occupation. Their principal problem had been loneliness, since neither of them spoke Cree or French. They stressed that they never had to walk, that they had ridden in the Pritchards' wagon; once or twice they had walked off together when their cart was not ready, but they had never been compelled to walk. In fact, John Pritchard had made his children walk so that the two might ride. Mrs. Delaney stated that:

> Pritchard and all the Breeds walked always, though by making us walk they could have ridden. His two little boys, aged thirteen and fifteen, walked, though their feet

---

62   Sharpe, "Unspeakable Limits," 33.

63   *Minneapolis Pioneer Press,* June 25, 1885; *Toronto Evening News,* June 9, 1885; *Globe,* June 23, 1885; and *Montreal Daily Star,* June 23, 1885.

became very sore at times, but they never complained, because they knew their walking enabled us to ride. They were noble little fellows.[64]

The two women reserved their highest praise for John Pritchard, Adolphus Nolin, and Pierre Blondin. They were all credited, but especially Pritchard, with having saved them from suffering and hardship, as well as the menacing behaviour of some Plains Cree men. According to the women Pritchard and Nolin had each given the Cree a horse for Mrs. Delaney, and Pierre Blondin had given two horses for Mrs. Gowanlock. From time to time Pritchard and Nolin had also given up other possessions such as blankets and dishes. Mrs. Delaney had some critical words to say about the administration of Indian Affairs. According to one correspondent, she laid at Lieutenant Governor (and former Indian Commissioner) Edgar Dewdney's door "the greatest portion of the blame for the Indians' antipathy to the instructors, and to his door, a share in the causes that led to the massacre."[65] Theresa Delaney was reported as saying that on his visits to Frog Lake Dewdney made many promises and raised expectations that were unfulfilled.

Changing and Contested Stories of Captivity

After hearing so many stories of the nameless horrors that the women had been subjected to, and having just invested so much in the costly military campaign against what was understood to be a Métis and Indian insurrection, it was difficult for many in the non-Aboriginal public to accept the women's initial statements that they had been treated well, and that they were particularly grateful to Métis men and their families. Much of the later stages of the campaign had been understood as a crusade to save the white women. English- as well as French-speaking soldiers had literally "tramped the soles off their boots" to reach the women and avenge their treatment. These were the heroic rescuers, not Métis such as Pritchard, who after all were the "enemy." Criticism of government was not entirely welcomed either, as the campaign was about maintaining and consolidating Canada's hold over the West. The women's accounts contained many shades of gray, rather than the simplistic dichotomy of dark villains and white heroes, and this was not what the hour called for.

John Pritchard soon became the focus of media attention, and his reputation was increasingly sullied, his motives questioned. When news of the women's safe return first became public there was some talk of a reward for Pritchard and Blondin. In the June 18 *Week* of Toronto it was declared that a woman had proposed:

> every one of her sex who is able to do so should contribute twenty-five cents with which to form a fund to reward the men by whom the liberty of the captives was purchased. Should the sisterhood act upon the suggestion, John Pritchard and Pierre Blondin will not go unrewarded.

---

64   Part of a deposition given by Mrs. Delaney was quoted at length in C.P. Mulvaney, *The History of the North-West Rebellion of 1885* (Toronto: A.H. Hovey & Co., 1885), 405.

65   *Globe,* July 7, 1885.

But there emerged a strong campaign to impugn Pritchard, and to terminate all efforts to reward him or any other Métis. At the forefront of this campaign was the Reverend Dr. Hooper of Kingston, who was strident and vocal in his claim that Pritchard and other Métis men had only purchased the women for their own vile purposes, and "were only defeated in their intentions by the resolute conduct of their victims. Foiled in their base plans they made literal slaves of them during their captivity."[66] Pritchard was obliged to defend himself against these and other charges that he had stolen goods, and on August 8, 1885 he published a letter in the *Toronto Daily Mail*. Pritchard also had his defenders. In an editorial in the *Edmonton Bulletin* of August 18 it was stressed that Pritchard had sacrificed a great deal in the cause of humanity, and deserved a reward as well as to have his horses and property returned to him:

> Pritchard behaved like a man, in the case, and deserves the title of hero far more than many another who has received it by general acclamation. To their credit may it said many of the women of Canada desired to recognize in a substantial manner his chivalrous action, but unfortunately were deterred therefrom by some blackguard, said to have reverend prefixed to his name, raising a false report concerning him.

Despite his supporters, Pritchard never did receive a reward, compensation, pension or recognition.

As the debate over Pritchard's motives indicates, the experiences of the two women continued to be a battleground long after they emerged from the Cree camp, with some interpreting good treatment, and others seeing harsh treatment. In a newspaper such as the Regina *Leader*, that wished to congratulate the wisdom of government administration, it was stated that the fact that all of the prisoners had been restored without being ill-treated "shows that the past policy of kindness to the Indians has not been in vain … the way Big Bear's band treated Mrs. Gowanlock and Mrs. Delaney shows the civilizing influence of kindness." On the other hand were editorials such as those of P.G. Laurie of the Battleford *Saskatchewan Herald*. Like the owner of the *Leader*, Laurie was a strong Conservative, so simple party lines do not account for conflicting opinions. He took great exception to any complimentary statements about the treatment of the women. "Big Bear," he wrote, "had sold the unfortunate women just as he would horses, regardless of what fate might be in store for them," and it was heartless to say "that two months imprisonment of these ladies in the camp of savages is neither injury nor ill treatment."[67] It was this latter highly negative view of the women's two months that began to take centre stage as June gave way to July.

Mrs. Gowanlock and Mrs. Delaney spent two weeks in Battleford, and then left for Eastern Canada. At many of the stops along the route they were greeted by crowds of well-wishers, and the journey was detailed in the press at every stopover. The women

---

66 *Macleod Gazette*, July 21, 1885.

67 *Saskatchewan Herald*, July 6, 1885.

took the train to Port Arthur and then went by steamer to Owen Sound. As they walked down the gangway of the steamer they were met by Andrew Gowanlock, Theresa's brother-in-law, who accompanied them to Toronto which they reached on July 13. As mentioned earlier, the Gowanlock brothers owned the *Parkdale Times* Newspaper, Book and Publishing Company.

Two Months in the Camp of Big Bear

There could be many possible reasons why the book *Two Months* was produced, and so quickly. There was a high degree of public interest in the story of the two women. They were approached by agents, bureaus and even ministers to take to the lecture platform. The Gowanlock brothers may have hoped to profit from a book that detailed the experiences of the two women who had captivated the nation, and perhaps it was hoped that the book might provide some income for the authors. The women authors likely wished to make it very clear that the rumours of the spring were not true; they had not been made to suffer the "fate worse than death." Such a cloud hanging over them would have made it difficult for them to function socially upon their return to the East. But there may have been other pressures as well. According to some descendants of Mrs. Delaney's family, she was pressured into preparing her account by the Gowanlock family, and both women were reluctant to criticize government actions or policies for fear of jeopardizing their chances of receiving government pensions.[68] Mrs. Delaney received her government pension by Order-in-Council dated November 14, 1885 (the day before Riel went to the gallows), while Mrs. Gowanlock received a settlement from the Commission on Rebellion Losses as well as a pension, although this was not granted until 1888.[69] It is interesting to compare these pensions with that of Jane Quinn, also a widow of Frog Lake, who had a daughter to support. While Mrs. Delaney received $400 dollars a year, Jane Quinn was granted a mere $12 a month, "upon the understanding that she would lead a moral life." For a time Jane Quinn lived in Montana, and upon her return to southern Alberta in 1912 she applied for her pension. The chief of police at Fort Macleod had to first report on whether she was leading a moral life, and when he found her to be a "hard working woman with a good reputation in the district," her pension was resumed. Cheque no. 4540 for $12 arrived at Macleod on the day Mrs. Quinn died in January 1913.[70]

The stories presented in *Two Months* differ in significant respects from some of the statements the women made immediately upon their release. Overall the book stresses the "untold suffering and privations" that they had to endure at the hands of

---

68   Hughes, *The Frog Lake "Massacre,"* 1.

69   NA, RG 10, vol. 3719, file 22-649, L. Vankoughnet to Sir John A. Macdonald, July 24, 1885, and Order-in-Council, November 14, 1885; and N.O Cote, controller, to W.W. Cory, deputy minister of the Interior, May 5, 1915.

70   NA, RG 10, vol. 3831, file 63891, assistant deputy and secretary to W.J. Hyde, October 7, 1912, and E. Foster Brown to Department of Indian Affairs, January 20, 1913.

"savages." The women are prostrated by their bereavement, by fatigue and by "the constant dread of outrage and death." They endure "physical pains, dangers, colds, heats, sleepless nights, long marches, scant food, poor raiment."[71] They are constantly made to walk, and are worked to death. While Pritchard is praised and thanked by both women, there are also hints throughout that the Pritchards were nonetheless not entirely trustworthy. Pierre Blondin and Gregory Donaire are two Métis who are especially vilified, despite the fact that the women had initially voiced their appreciation for Blondin in particular. There is also very little that could be interpreted as criticism of government administration. Mrs. Delaney emphasized in her section of *Two Months* that the Indians were treated with generosity and kindness, and had no grievances or complaints. The true villain in her account was the HBC. While the government wished to enlighten and civilize, the company wished to keep Aboriginal people in a state of "savagery," as hunters and trappers rather than peaceful agriculturalists. She claimed that rebellion served the interests of the HBC.

How and why did *Two Months* come to project this particular version of events? As mentioned above, the women's need to acquire pensions probably caused them to mute any criticism they might have of government administration. It is also possible that *Two Months* represents their reflections on their experiences in a much more sustained way than permitted in their initial statements. Perhaps their original statements reflected the immediacy of their experiences, their need to survive in that world, whereas they began to feel differently looking back after weeks and months. (The "Stockholm Syndrome" is the term used today to explain the behaviour of hostages or prisoners who appear to accept and replicate the behaviour of their captors.[72])

Two Months also conformed to the conventions of the classic Indian captivity narrative, and this form had an influence over the way in which the story was presented. From the seventeenth century, Indian captivity narratives were a popular form of literature in North America, particularly in the United States. Today there is an enormous body of literature that analyzes and interprets these narratives.[73] These studies indicate that care must be taken in making broad generalizations about the narratives, as there were many different kinds, and certain themes dominated at certain periods, according to the major preoccupations of the day.[74] But the typical American Indian captivity narrative of the late nineteenth century was essentially a device for anti-Indian propaganda. They functioned to sustain the established

---

71   *Two Months*, 119.

72   Christopher Castiglia, *Bound and Determined: Captivity, Culture-Crossing, and White Woman-hood from Mary Rowlandson to Patty Hearst* (Chicago: University of Chicago Press, 1996), 98.

73   The most comprehensive book is June Namias, *White Captives: Gender and Ethnicity on the American Frontier* (Chapel Hill, University of North Carolina Press, 1993).

74   Colin Calloway (ed.), *North Country Captives: Selected Narratives of Indian Captivity from Vermont and New Hampshire* (Hanover, NH: University Press of New England, 1992).

hierarchies of race and gender. There was a reasonably consistent structure to the narrative, similar rhetorical devices and illustrations. They generally told the story of an innocent captive who was doing his or her best to establish "civilization" in a bountiful wilderness. They could be about men or women, but captivity narratives were especially useful when the protagonists were women, as they appeared more vulnerable than the male captive. By the late nineteenth century, a culture of delicate and frail white femininity prevailed, and the loss of a protective husband supposedly left a woman totally defenceless. The death of the husband was the key event in the narrative, and the survivors were plunged into an alien world, experiencing great suffering until the heroic rescue by white males. Throughout the narrative the white woman's weakness and vulnerablity is stressed, which helps to define and highlight white masculine strength and courage. Aboriginal males and females are the reverse or negative images of their white counterparts. Aboriginal women, for example, are inevitably presented as drudges, or beasts or burden, mistreated within their own society. This forms a sharp contrast to the "tenderly reared," and delicate white women captives. Captivity narratives inevitably included an illustration of such mistreatment of Aboriginal women intended to starkly depict this contrast. Aboriginal males were cast as brutal threats to the virtue of white women, and as savage not chivalrous warriors. With the heroic rescue of white women captives, law and order is restored. The captives gratefully return to patriarchal protection. The future of the nation, not of individuals, has been at stake and has been rescued. In the United States captivity narratives helped to establish and to sustain boundaries between indigenous people and the evolving community of the American nation. The narrators inevitably only reluctantly agree to write about their experiences; the women especially claim only an indifferent education but they promise a plain and unvarnished tale.

Captivity narratives were not unique to the United States. Narratives of the captivity of white women at the hands of "barbarous savages" are a structure embedded within the colonial experience of Australia, South Africa, and a great many other colonial settings.[75] Eliza Fraser, shipwrecked off Australia in 1836, is a good example. She spent six weeks with the Aborigines on what is known today as Fraser Island. She gave different reports of her ordeal to different audiences, and in her initial statements there was no mention of the savagery and barbarism that found its way into subsequent accounts; she displayed limited sympathy for her captors, and

---

75 Kay Schaffer, *In the Wake of First Contact: The Eliza Fraser Stories* (Cambridge: Cambridge University Press, 1995). See also Kay Schaffer, "Colonizing Gender in Colonial Australia: The Eliza Fraser Story," in Alison Blunt and Gilllian Rose (eds.), *Writing Women and Space: Colonial and Postcolonial Geographies* (New York: Guilford Press, 1994): 101-20; and Kay Schaffer, "'We Are Like Eliza': Twentieth-Century Australian Responses to the Eliza Fraser Saga," in Ian J. McNiven, Lynette Russell and Kay Schaffer (eds.), *Constructions of Colonialism: Perspectives on Eliza Fraser's Shipwreck* (London and New York: Leicester University Press, 1998): 79-96.

acknowledged their kindnesses to her. The published account was a sensationalized captivity narrative with fabricated tales of torture and cannibalism. As Kay Shaffer has argued, knowlege about Eliza Fraser was manipulated in order to regulate race, class and gender relations, and to maintain dominant ideologies of colonialism and Victorian morality. Eliza Fraser's original testimony was transformed in order to regulate the borders between "civilization and savagery."

There were also Indian captivity narratives that took place in Canada, although never in the numbers produced in the United States.[76] While captivity narratives from the American West flourished in the mid- to later nineteenth century, there were almost none from Western Canada, *Two Months* being almost the sole exception.[77] One American captivity narrative that was exceptionally popular at this time in Canada however was Fanny Kelly's *Narrative of My Captivity Among the Sioux Indians*, originally published in 1871.[78] Canadians claimed Mrs. Kelly as one of their own as she was born near Orillia. There were apparently four Canadian editions of this book, and in introductions that were different from the American editions, the clear message was that such a refined and carefully reared lady would never fall into the hands of "merciless savages" in Canada. Mrs. Kelly's account of atrocities in this case served to turn public opinion not only against the Indians, but against the Americans, who were not as enlightened and benevolent as Canadians. Captivity narratives, then, must be read very critically and used with great caution.

The stories of Mrs. Gowanlock and Mrs. Delaney were in many ways transformed, embellished and embroidered in order to conform to the expectations of the nineteenth century Indian captivity narrative. The authors promise truthful and accurate accounts, making it clear that they do not possess or aspire to literary excellence. This is the story of inexplicable brutality against innocent, virtuous people who "left comfortable homes in the east in order to carry civilization into the remote places of the west."[79] Frog Lake is extolled as a beautiful and enchanting location, and there is great praise for the West as a potential home for industrious

---

76 See, for example, John Demos, *The Unredeemed Captive: A Family Story from Early America*, (New York: Alfred A. Knopf, 1994).

77 There are two other captivity narratives from Western Canada: H. Stewart (ed.), *The Adventures and Sufferings of John R. Jewitt: Captive of the Maquinna* (Vancouver: Douglas & McIntyre, 1987), and E. James (ed.), *A Narrative of the Captivity and Adventure of John Tanner During Thirty Years Residence Among the Indians in the Interior of North America* (Minneapolis: Ross and Haines Inc., 1956).

78 Fanny Kelly, *Narrative of My Captivity Among the Sioux Indians* (Toronto: Maclear, 1872). Although I have located a first and a fourth Canadian edition of this book (Toronto: Maclear, 1878) which seems to be sometimes catalogued as "Queen of the Sioux," I have not been able to find any copies of the second and third editions. Thanks to Donald Smith at the University of Calgary Department of History for first bringing Fanny Kelly to my attention.

79 *Two Months*, 43.

white farmers. Yet this tranquil and prosperous settlement is destroyed. The weak and vulnerable women survivors, prostrated by fatigue and exposure, are subjected to untold suffering. There are obligatory passages on Indian customs and manners, particularly in Mrs. Gowanlock's section, containing a sampling of the dominant stereotypes of the day. Just as the darkest hour is that which proceeds dawn, the women believed they faced certain death just before their escape and rescue. There are odes to the brave men from Eastern Canada who sacrificed so much to come to their assistance. The women return to the sacred precincts of the paternal hearth. In her conclusion, Mrs. Gowanlock provides a panoramic view of her experiences, emphasizing once again how sinister Blondin was, and how she had to witness numerous heart-rending scenes, such as the desecration of her husband's body (a sight she likely did not see). In her conclusion, Mrs. Delaney makes a direct reference to the great nation that she predicts will grow from these struggles, dangers and tempests.

Yet there are occasions in *Two Months* when the authors break free of conventions and expectations. Mrs. Gowanlock acknowledges the kindnesses of some Aboriginal people, particularly women. In her description of "Indian boys" she breaks free for a moment from her very negative descriptions to say that they took delight in picking the prettiest flowers for her. She also makes it clear that Big Bear wanted peace, and that he did not have control over some of his men. Mrs. Delaney also at times challenges the conventions of the genre. She insists that Pritchard was "A TRULY GOOD MAN," the only time that such emphasis is given.

The kind of illustrations featured in *Two Months* were common to American Indian captivity narratives of the late nineteenth century. The image of Aboriginal women as "Beasts of Burden" was particularly common, and very often a dog was included to show that they were treated in the same way (see page 7). This was intended to symbolize what was seen as the central shortcoming of Aboriginal society; that women were treated brutally, quite in contrast to the supposed elevated and cherished status of white women. Other illustrations common to captivity narratives were those of happy, peaceful and bountiful settlements. The drawings of Frog Lake in *Two Months*, by F.W. Sutherland, bear little resemblance to the actual terrain (see page 60). Some of the illustrations were taken from those published more widely in 1885, particularly in the *Canadian Pictorial and Illustrated War News*. A drawing of Big Bear (not at all a likeness, see page 12), and of General Strange, appeared in other 1885 publications. Certain of these drawings were selected, and others excluded. An *Illustrated War News* drawing that was not included in *Two Months* showed John Pritchard in a heroic light, guarding an open tent in which we know the women are housed, while he keeps a steady eye on the Indian camp in the background.[80] The drawing of Theresa Delaney in *Two Months* bears striking resemblance to the picture of Fanny Kelly that appeared on the frontispiece of the many editions of her book.

---

80   *Canadian Pictorial and Illustrated War News*, July 4, 1885.

The pose, dress and hairstyle are remarkably similar, and in the absence of photographs of Mrs. Delaney it is possible that Fanny Kelly became the model for the drawing. (As an example of the kind of "borrowing" that went on, most of the illustrations from Fanny Kelly's book appeared in Edmund Collins, *The Story of Louis Riel: The Rebel Chief*, although with different captions, and no acknowledgement.[81])

Two Months was published in November 1885, the same month that Louis Riel was hanged in Regina (November 15) and eight males were hanged at Battleford (November 27), among whom were those found guilty of the Frog Lake murders. The perspective presented in the two women's narratives would have helped steel resolve that this public spectacle of repression of indigenous people was the best and most obvious course. Public opinion was divided on the hanging not only of Riel, but also of the eight Aboriginal men. In the editorials of several of the eastern newspapers, the wholesale execution of eight people was condemned as a sight unworthy of a civilized nation, and as carrying bloodthirstiness too far. The *Montreal Herald* called for the hangings to be postponed indefinitely in favour of life imprisonment, stating that "the proposal to give the public an exhibition of wholesale hanging is terribly repulsive to all humane persons…"[82] By being released at this time, and serialized in a paper such as the *Huron Expositor*, *Two Months* kept the issue of Frog Lake, and especially indignities to white women, before the reading public.

After 1885 there was a shift in the attitudes of Euro-Canadians toward Aboriginal people. While there had been limited tolerance and understanding of their situation before, after 1885 they were viewed as threats to the property, safety and prosperity of the white settlers. One Methodist missionary called for the removal of all Indians to a province north and east of Lake Winnipeg, as 1885 had destroyed the confidence of the white settlers, and peace and contentment could never be attained if the reserves remained scattered throughout.[83] A removal policy was not adopted, but as in other colonial settings where acts of resistance were met with extremely harsh retribution, repressive measures were introduced in the Canadian West. Also as in other colonial settings, protecting white women became a pretext for suppressing and controlling the indigenous population. An 1886 government pamphlet stressed that measures were necessary; otherwise white women might once again be dragged into horrible captivity.[84] Whole bands that were declared "disloyal" had their arms, ammunition, horses, and even items such as matches removed. New policies were pursued, such as a pass system, that aimed at rigidly monitoring and controlling the lives of people on

---

81 Edmund Collins, *The Story of Louis Riel: The Rebel Chief* (Toronto: J.S. Robertson and Brothers, 1885).

82 *Montreal Herald and Daily Commercial Gazette*, November 19, 1885.

83 E.R. Young, "The Indian Problem," *Canadian Methodist Magazine and Review* (June 1885): 465-69.

84 *The Facts Respecting Indian Administration in the North-West* (Ottawa: Department of Indian Affairs: 1886).

reserves.[85] The major goal of Indian affairs administrators after 1885 was to disband, break up, and assimilate what was seen as a "foreign element" in the midst of the nation.[86] *Two Months* helped to define the indigenous residents as the "foreign element," and to establish white women as the "civilizers" who would create and uphold the moral and cultural environment of the nation to take shape. Boundaries between Aboriginal people and newcomers had to be clarified and maintained if the West was to be home for white women.

Photographs

1. Theresa Gowanlock (Saskatchewan Archives Board R-B13140; National Archives of Canada C028218)

2. Big Bear (Saskatchewan Archives Board R-A6276)

3. Thomas Quinn (Saskatchewan Archives Board R-A5093)

4. Graves of the victims of Frog Lake, taken by Geraldine Moodie, c. 1895 (RCMP Museum, Regina, 941.9.52)

---

85 See Carter, *Lost Harvests*, chapter 4, "Assault Upon the "Tribal" System: Government Policy After 1885," 130-58.

86 Ibid., 146.

Part 1
Being the Story
of Theresa Gowanlock

INTRODUCTION

*I*t is not the desire of the author of this work to publish the incidents which drenched a peaceful and prosperous settlement in blood, and subjected the survivors to untold suffering and privations at the hands of savages, in order to gratify a morbid craving for notoriety. During all my perils and wanderings amid the snow and ice of that trackless prairie, the hope that nerved me to struggle on, was, that if rescued, I might within the sacred precincts of the paternal hearth, seek seclusion, where loving hands would help me to bear the burden of my sorrow, and try to make me forget at times, if they could not completely efface from my memory, the frightful scenes enacted around that prairie hamlet, which bereft me of my loved one, leaving my heart and fireside desolate for ever. Prostrated by fatigue and exposure, distracted by the constant dread of outrage and death, I had well-nigh abandoned all hope of ever escaping from the Indians with my life, but, as the darkness of the night is just before the dawn, so my fears which had increased until I was in despair, God in his inscrutable way speedily calmed, for while I was brooding over and preparing for my impending fate, a sudden commotion attracted my attention and in less time than it takes to write it, I was free. From that moment I received every kindness and attention, and as I approached the confines of civilization, I became aware of how diligently I had been sought after, and that for weeks I had been the object of the tenderest solicitude, not only of my friends and relations, but of the whole continent.

There have appeared so many conflicting statements in the public press regarding my capture and treatment while with the Indians, that it is my bounden duty to give to the public a truthful and accurate description of my capture, detention and misfortunes while captive in the camp of Big Bear. The task may be an irksome one and I might with justice shrink from anything which would recall the past. Still it is a debt of gratitude I owe to the people of this broad dominion. To the brave men who sacrificed their business and comfort and endured the hardships incident to a soldier's life, in order to vindicate the law. And to the noble men and women who planned for the comfort and supplied the wants of the gallant band who had so nobly responded to the call of duty and cry for help. And I gladly embrace this opportunity of showing to the public and especially the ladies, my appreciation of their kindness and sympathy in my bereavement, and their noble and disinterested efforts for my release. In undertaking a task which has no pleasures for me, and has been accomplished under the most trying difficulties and with the greatest physical suffering, I have embodied in the narrative a few of the manners and customs of Indians, the leading features of the country, only sufficient to render it clear and intelligible. I make no apology for issuing this volume to the public as their unabated interest make it manifest that they desire it, and I am only repaying a debt of gratitude by giving a truthful narrative to correct false impressions, for their kindness and sympathy to me.

I trust the public will receive the work in the spirit in which it is given and any literary defects which it may have, and I am sure there are many, may be overlooked, as I am only endeavoring to rectify error, instead of aspiring to literary excellence. I express my sincere and heartfelt thanks to the half-breeds who befriended me during my captivity, and to the friends and public generally who sheltered and assisted me in many ways and by many acts of kindness and sympathy, and whose attention was unremitting until I had reached my destination.

And now I must bid the public a grateful farewell and seek my wished for seclusion from which I would never have emerged but to perform a public duty.

Theresa Gowanlock

ONE

We Leave Ontario

$\mathcal{W}$e left my father's house at Tintern on the 7th of October, 1884, having been married on the 1st, for Parkdale, where we spent a few days with my husband's friends. We started for our home on the 10th by the Canadian Pacific Railway to Owen Sound, thence by boat to Port Arthur, and then on to Winnipeg by rail, where we stopped one night, going on the next day to Regina. We only stopped in that place one day, taking rail again to Swift Current, arriving there the same day. This ended our travel by the locomotion of steam.

After taking in a supply of provisions we made a start for Battleford, distant 195 miles, by buckboard over the prairie, which stretches out about 130 miles in length, and for the remaining 55 miles there are clumps of trees or bluffs as they are called, scattered here and there. Our journey over this part was very pleasant, the weather was fine and the mode of travelling, which was new to me, delightful. Our company, consisted in addition to ourselves, of only one person, Mr. Levalley, a gentleman from Ottawa. We passed four nights under canvas. The journey was not a lonely one, the ships of the prairie were continually on the go, we passed several companies of freighters with harnessed oxen, half-breeds and Indians. It was also full of incident and adventure; on one occasion, when cooking our tea, we set fire to the prairie, although we worked hard to put it out, it in a very few minutes spread in a most alarming manner, and entirely beyond our control, and we let it go looking on enjoying the scene. Upon nearing Battleford a number of half-famished squaws came to us begging for something to eat, but we were not in a position, unfortunately, to supply their wants, on account of our larder having run dry. We entered Battleford on the 19th of October.

The town of Battleford is situated on the Battle river. The old on one side, the new on the other, in the direction of the fort. When the Indians plundered that place it was the town on the south bank. The houses on the opposite bank were protected by the guns at the fort. My husband had a store on the north bank in the direction of the fort.

The town is very scattered, covering a large area of ground, it is verily a place of distances and quite in keeping with the north-west generally. There are a few fine houses in the place, notably, the industrial home for Indian children and the residence of Judge Rolleau.

TWO

Incidents at Battleford

Ⓘ remained at Battleford six weeks, while my husband went to Frog Creek, (where he had thirteen men working on the house and mills,) and while there I became initiated into the manners and customs of the inhabitants. A few incidents which happened during my stay might be interesting to the reader, therefore, I will jot them down as they come to mind.

After our arrival the Indians and squaws came to see me and would go and tell some of the others to come and see the monias, (squaw) and when they saw my husband they asked him why he did not live with her, and if she was well; and one day I walked with him over to where he was keeping store before he went west and the Indians came in and shook hands, and laughed, and the squaws thought my costume was rather odd and not in keeping with that of the fashionable north-western belle. The squaws cut off about three yards of print and make the skirt; while others take flour sacks and cut holes through for the waist and have leggings and moccasins; they would disdain to wear such an article as hose.

They are quite adepts [*sic*] in the art of tanning. I saw them tanning leather; they took the skin and put something on it, I do not know what it was, and put it in the sun for a few days, then with a small sharp iron fastened on a long handle, they scraped the skin with this until very smooth, and greased it over and put it in the sun again for some time, afterwards two squaws pulled it until nice and soft, and then it was ready for use.

One afternoon I was out shopping and on my way home I saw some little Indian children coasting down hill on an earthen plate, but before getting to the end of the hill, to their evident surprise the plate broke and they commenced crying because it was broken and went back and got another one, and so on until they thought they would try tin plates, and the little friend that was with me, Effie Laurie, took the tin plate from them and sat down on it herself and went down the hill, and they looked so astonished to think that a white woman would do such a thing.

Another time on going out while two men were crossing the bridge over Battle river; a horse broke through and was killed and the squaws gathered around it taking the skin off, while others carried some of the carcass away, and I asked what they were going to do with it, and my husband said "they will take it home and have a big feast

Beasts of Burden

and if the meat has been poisoned they will boil it for a long time, changing the water, and in this way anything that was poisonous would not affect them."

The way the Indians get their wood, they send their squaws to the bush to cut the wood and they take a rope and tie around as much as they can carry, and hang it on their backs. Those who have dogs to carry the wood for them tie two long sticks together, fastening them on the dog's back, then tying a large bundle of wood on the back part of the cross sticks by that means the squaw is relieved from the task. The squaws perform all manual labor, while the big, lazy, good-for-nothing Indian lolls about in idleness.

THREE

On to Our Home

At the end of six weeks my husband returned from the west, and with many pleasant recollections of Battleford, we left for our own home, which I had pictured in my mind with joyous anticipation, as the place of our continued happiness; a beautiful oasis, in that land of prairie and sparse settlement, and with a buoyancy of spirit which true happiness alone can bring, I looked forward with anticipated pleasure, which made that little log house appear to me, a palace, and we its king and queen.

On this last part of our journey we were favored with the company of Mr. Ballentyne of Battleford who went with us, and after the first day's travelling, we stopped all night at a half-breed's house, where they had a large fire-place made of mud, which was just like a solid piece of stone; they had a bright fire, and everything appeared nice and tidy within; a woman was making bannock, and when she had the dough prepared, she took a frying pan and put the cake in and stood it up before the fire. This is the way they do all their baking, and then she fried some nice white fish and hung a little kettle on a long iron hook over the fire, put in potatoes, and boiled the tea-kettle, making the tea in it too. She then spread a white cloth over the table and we all enjoyed our supper together after the long ride. The squaw gave us a nice clean bed to sleep in, making theirs on the floor and in the morning I saw four little children crawling out from under the bed where we slept, and my husband looked up at me and laughed, and said, "that is where children sleep up in *this country*." Their ways appeared very strange to me, and in the morning before going away, they gave us a warm breakfast.

We travelled all the next day and camped that night. We had a small tin stove which is part of a camping outfit, and which smoked very much while cooking. We had great trouble to know how we would obtain a light, but we had a candle and we lighted that, and then we had nothing to hold it in, but as necessity is the mother of invention, we found a way out of the difficulty; we took a pocket knife that had two blades, and stuck one blade in the tent pole and opened the other half way, fastening the candle into the blade, which answered the purpose and enabled us to see while we ate our supper. We then turned down our beds, and in a few minutes were fast asleep. When morning came we had breakfast, and travelled on again. Mr. Ballentyne shot some prairie chickens and we had them for our dinner, which was a great treat to me.

We arrived at Fort Pitt on the tenth, bidding Mr. Ballentyne good-bye, stopped at Mr. McLean's all night, where we enjoyed a very pleasant evening.

The next morning we left for Onion Lake, where we were welcomed by Mr. Mann and family, and after a night's rest proceeded on our journey to Frog Lake, reaching there on the 12th. We went to Mr. and Mrs. Delaney's, who kindly allowed me to stop there until my husband fixed up some articles of furniture at our own house two miles further on and south-west of the Lake.

After arriving at Mrs. Delaney's, my husband left me and went down to the house to work; on Saturday evening he came back. On Sunday morning Mr. Quinn came over and asked us to go for a drive, we accepted the invitation. It was a bright frosty morning; he took us to our little home that I had not yet seen. On hearing the men singing who were employed at the mill, we drove down to their cooking tent, where we found Mr. Gilchrist cooking breakfast for fourteen men. They had a large cooking stove inside, with a long board table; the table was covered with tin plates and cups. They had rabbit soup, and bread and coffee for breakfast; after getting ourselves warm we drove back to Mr. Delaney's. On the following Thursday my husband drove up and took me to our home, where all was in beautiful order, and Mr. Gilchrist waiting for our arrival.

FOUR

At Home

*N*ow we are at home and I am thankful. There they nestle in a pretty valley, the simple house, the store, and beside the brook, the mill. The music of the workman's hammer alone breaks the stillness that pervades the scene, and the hills send back the echo without a discordant note. The hills were covered with trees, principally poplar and spruce, interspersed with berry-bearing shrubs. A most beautiful and enchanting location.

That little settlement of our own was situated upon Frog Creek, about three miles west of the lake of the same name, and distant from the Frog Lake Settlement, our nearest white neighbours, about two miles. But we had neighbours close by, who came in to see us the next day, shaking hands and chatting to us in Cree, of which language we knew but little. The Indians appeared to be very kind and supplied us with white fish twice a week which they procured from the river for which in return we gave sugar, tea, prints, &c., from the store. Christmas and New Year's were celebrated in about the same manner that they are amongst us civilized people. Both Indians and squaws put on their good clothes, which at the best of times is very scant, and do their calling. They salute the inmates of each house they enter with a congratulatory shake, expecting to be kissed in return. Just think of having to kiss a whole tribe of Indians in one day, that part we would rather do by proxy. We would not countenance it in any way.

On Christmas day we went out for a walk along Frog Creek; on our way we came to where two little Indian children were catching rabbits with a snare, they stepped to one side and let us pass, and were delighted to have us watching them while catching their game; and further on some of the squaws had holes cut in the ice, and having a sharp hook were catching fish. In this way they get fish all winter, and to look at these "shrimpy-looking" women trotting along with their brown babies slung in a sort of loose pocket dangling away behind their backs, it was comical in the extreme, they would stop and look and laugh at us, our appearance being so very different to their own dark skin and sharp eyes. They wear their hair hanging, strung with brass beads, and have small pieces of rabbit fur tied in; and the men wear theirs cut very short in front, hanging over their brows, and ornaments of every description. These people don't set at table on chairs, rich or poor; they squat down on their feet in a fashion that would soon tire us exceedingly. Then at night they wrap themselves up in a

The Home of Mr. and Mrs. J.A. Gowanlock

blanket, lie down and sleep as soundly as we would in our warm feather bed and blankets.

My husband and the men worked hard during the next two months on the mill in order to get it finished before the spring set in. As far as the weather was concerned it was very favourable for working. The men lost no time from the cold. During that period the thermometer ranged from zero to 60° below but the air was so clear and bracing that the cold was never felt. I have experienced more severe weather in Ontario than I ever did in this part. I have heard of north-west blizzards, but they are confined to the prairie and did not reach us. It is the most beautiful country I ever saw with its towering hills, majestic rivers, beautiful flowers and rolling land. I had made up my mind to see nothing but frost, ice and snow, but was agreeably disappointed.

Nothing of an eventful nature transpired, during those two months, the mill was about completed and Williscraft and the other men were discharged with the exception of Mr. Gilchrist, who assisted my husband. The machinery was all in position and everything done but finishing up, when on the 17th of March, two men, strangers, made their appearance at the mill and asked for employment. They said they were weary and worn and had left Duck Lake in order to avoid the trouble that was brewing there. One was Gregory Donaire and the other Peter Blondin, my husband took pity on them and gave them employment. They worked for us until the massacre. They were continually going too and fro among the Indians, and I cannot but believe, that they were cognizant of everything that was going on, if not responsible in a great degree for the murders which were afterwards committed.

FIVE

Wood and Plain Indians

*T*he Indians are in their habits very unclean and filthy. They will not in the least impress anyone to such an extent that they would be willing to forego the restrictions of civilized life, and enter upon the free life of the red man.

The Indians living on the reserve in the neighbourhood of Frog Creek are known as the Wood Crees, they were all peaceable and industrious, and were becoming proficient in the art of husbandry. They lived in the log cabins in the winter, but in the summer they took to their tents. They numbered about 200 persons. They appeared satisfied with their position which was much better than what falls to the lot of other Indians. They did not take part in the massacre, nor where [*sic*] they responsible for it in any way.

The Plain Crees are composed of the worst characters from all the tribes of that name. They were dissatisfied, revengeful, and cruel, they could not be persuaded to select their reserve until lately, and then they would not settle upon it. Their tastes lay in a direction the opposite to domestic; they were idle and worthless, and were the Indians who killed our dear ones on that ever to be remembered 2nd of April. Those same Indians were constantly fed by Mr. Delaney and my husband. The following correspondence will show how he treated those ungrateful characters: — Big Bear's Indians were sent up to Frog Lake, it is said, by Governer Dewdney who told them, if they would go there, they would never be hungry, but last winter their rations were stopped, and they had to work to get provisions, or starve. They would go around to the settlers' houses and ask for something to eat, and Mr. Delaney would give those Indians rations, paying for them out of his own salary. Gov.

Big Bear

Dewdney wrote a letter stating that he must stop it at once; but he did not listen to him and kept on giving to them until the outbreak. And the very men he befriended were the ones who hurled him into sudden death.

Big Bear was only nominally the chief of this tribe, the ruling power being in the hands of Wandering Spirit, a bad and vicious man, who exercised it with all the craft and cunning of an accomplished freebooter.

Wandering Spirit

SIX

The Massacre

$\mathcal{N}$ ow come the dreadful scenes of blood and cruel death. The happy life is changed to one of suffering and sorrow. The few months of happiness I enjoyed with the one I loved above all others was abruptly closed — taken from me for ever — it was cruel, it was dreadful. When I look back to it all, I often wonder, is it all a dream, and has it really taken place. Yes, the dream is too true; it is a terrible reality, and as such will never leave my heart, or be effaced from off my mind.

The first news we heard of the Duck Lake affair was on the 30th of March. Mr. Quinn, the Indian Agent, at Frog Lake, wrote a letter to us and sent it down to our house about twelve o'clock at night with John Pritchard, telling my husband and I to go up to Mr. Delaney's on Tuesday morning, and with his wife go on to Fort Pitt, and if they saw any excitement they would follow. We did not expect anything to occur. When we got up to Mr. Delaney's we found the police had left for Fort Pitt. Big Bear's Indians were in the house talking to Mr. Quinn about the trouble at Duck Lake, and saying that Poundmaker the chief at Battleford wanted Big Bear to join him but he would not, as he intended remaining where he was and live peaceably. They considered Big Bear to be a better man than he was given credit for.

On the 1st of April they were in, making April fools of the white people and shaking hands, and they thought I was frightened and told me not to be afraid, because they would not hurt us. My husband left me at Mr. Delaney's and went back to his work at the mill, returning in the evening with Mr. Gilchrist. We all sat talking for some time along with Mr. Dill, who had a store at Frog Lake and Mr. Cameron, clerk for the Hudson Bay Company. We all felt perfectly safe where we were, saying that as we were so far away from the trouble at Duck Lake, the Government would likely come to some terms with them and the affair be settled at once. The young Chief and another Indian by the name of Isador said if anything was wrong among Big Bear's band they would come and tell us; and that night Big Bear's braves heard about it and watched them all night to keep them from telling us. We all went to bed not feeling in any way alarmed. About, five o'clock in the morning a rap came to the door and Mr. Delaney went down stairs and opened it, and John Pritchard and one of Big Bear's sons by the name of Ibesies were there.

Pritchard said "There trouble."

Mr. Delaney said "Where?"

Pritchard "*Here!* Our horses are all gone, the Indians deceived us, and said that some half-breeds from Edmonton had come in the night and had taken them to Duck Lake, but Big Bear's band has taken them and hid them, I am afraid it is all up."

My husband and I got up, and Mrs. Delaney came down stairs with a frightened look. In a few minutes Big Bear's Indians were all in the house, and had taken all the arms from the men saying they were going to protect us from the half-breeds, and then we felt we were being deceived. They took all the men over to Mr. Quinn's, and my husband and I were sitting on the lounge, and an Indian came in and took him by the arm saying he wanted him to go too; and he said to Mrs. Delaney and I "do not to be afraid, while I go with this Indian." We stopped in the house, and while they were gone some of the Indians came in and went through the cupboard to find something to eat. They opened the trap door to go down cellar, but it was very dark, and they were afraid to venture down. Then the men came back and Mrs. Delaney got breakfast. We all sat down, but I could not eat, and an Indian asked Mr. Gowanlock to tell me not to be afraid, they would not hurt us, and I should eat plenty. After breakfast they took us out of the house and escorted us over to the church; my husband taking my arm, Mr. and Mrs. Delaney were walking beside us. When we got to the church the priests were holding mass; it was Holy Thursday, and as we entered the door, Wandering Spirit sat on his knees with his gun; he was painted, and had on such a wicked look. The priests did not finish the service on account of the menacing manner of the Indians; they were both around and inside the church. We were all very much frightened by their behaviour. They then told us to go out of the church, and took us back to Mr. Delaney's, all the Indians going in too. We stopped there for awhile and an Indian came and told us to come out again, and my husband came to me and said "you had better put your shawl around you, for its [*sic*] very cold, perhaps we will not be gone long." We all went out with the Indians. They were going through all the stores. Everything was given to them, and they got everything they could wish for and took us up the hill towards their camp. We had only gone but a short distance from the house when we heard the reports of guns, but thought they were firing in the air to frighten us; but they had shot Quinn, Dill and Gilchrist, whom I did not see fall. Mr. and Mrs. Delaney were a short distance ahead of my husband, I having my husband's arm. Mr. Williscraft, an old grey-headed man about seventy-five years of age came running by us, and an Indian shot at him and knocked his hat off, and he turned around and said, "*Oh! don't shoot! don't shoot!*" But they fired again, and he ran screaming and fell in some bushes. On seeing, this I began crying, and my husband tried to comfort me, saying, "my *dear* wife be *brave* to the end," and irnmediately an Indian behind us fired, and my husband fell beside me his arm pulling from mine. I tried to assist him from falling. He put out his arms for me and fell, and I fell down beside him and buried my face on his, while his life was ebbing away so quickly, and was prepared for the next shot myself, thinking I was going with him too. But death just then was not ordained for me. I had yet to live. An Indian came and took me away from my dying husband [*sic*] side, and I refused to leave. Oh! to think of leaving my *dear* husband lying there for those cruel Indians to dance around. I begged of the

Indian to let me stay with him, but he took my arm and pulled me away. Just before this, I saw Mr. Delaney and a priest fall, and Mrs. Delaney was taken away in the same manner that I was. I still looking back to where my poor husband was lying dead; the Indian motioned to where he was going to take me, and on we went. I thought my heart would break; I would rather have died with my husband and been at rest.

"A rest that is sure for us all,
But sweeter to some."

The Scene of the Frog Lake Massacre

SEVEN

With the Indians

$\mathcal{H}$ardly knowing how I went or what I did, I trudged along in a half conscious condition. Led a captive into the camp of Big Bear by one of his vile band. Taken through brush and briar, a large pond came to view, we did not pass it by, he made me go through the water on that cold 2nd of April nearly to my waist. I got so very weak that I could not walk and the Indian pulled me along, in this way he managed to get me to his tepee. On seeing Mrs. Delaney taken away so far from me, I asked the Indian to take me to her; and he said "*No, No,*" and opening the tent shoved me in. A friendly squaw put down a rabbit robe for me to sit on; I was shivering with the cold; this squaw took my shoes and stockings off and partly dried them for me. Their tepees consisted of long poles covered with smoke-stained canvas with two openings, one at the top for a smoke hole and the other at the bottom for a door through which I had to crawl in order to enter. In the centre they have their fire; this squaw took a long stick and took out a large piece of beef from the kettle and offered it to me, which I refused, as I could not eat anything after what I had gone through.

Just then Big Bear's braves came into the tent; there were nearly thirty of them, covered with war paint, some having on my husband's clothes, and all giving vent to those terrible yells, and holding most murderous looking instruments. They were long wooden clubs. At one end were set three sharp shining knife blades. They all looked at me as I eyed those weapons (and they well matched the expression of their cruel mouths and develish [*sic*] eyes) thinking my troubles would soon be over I calmly awaited the result. But they sat down around me with a bottle full of something that looked like water, passing it from one Indian to the other, so I put on a brave look as if I was not afraid of them. After this they all went out and the most bloodcurdling yells that ever pierced my ears was their war-whoop, mingled with dancing and yelling and cutting most foolish antics.

I saw a little baby that I thought must be dead, lying in one part of the tent, they had it done up in a moss bag. I will try and give an idea of what it was like: they take a piece of cloth having it large at the top, and cut it around where the feet should be, and on both sides of this little bag they have loops of very fine leather, then they have a small thin cushion laid on this, the length of the child, and three or four pieces of different colored flannels, then they dress the baby in a thin print gown and put it in this bag, and its little legs are put down just as straight as a needle, covered over with moss, which they first heat very hot; then the arms are put down in the same way and the flannels are wrapped around very tight and then they lace the bag up, and all that can be seen is the little brown face peeping out.

Just then Pritchard's little girl came in where I was; she could talk a few words of English. I asked her where her pa was, and she said that he was putting up a tent not far away, and then I had some hope of getting from the Indians.

After I had been there for four hours, Louis Goulet and Andre Nault came in, and Goulet said to me "Mrs. Gowanlock if you will give yourself over to the half-breeds, they will not hurt you; Peter Blondin has gone down to where the mill is, and when he comes back he will give his horse for you." I asked them to interpret it to the Indians in order to let me go to Pritchard's tent for awhile, and the Indians said that she could go with this squaw. I went and was overjoyed to see Mrs. Delaney there also. After getting in there I was unconscious for a long time, and upon coming to my senses, I found Mrs. Pritchard bathing my face with cold water. When Blondin came back he gave his horse and thirty dollars for Mrs. Delaney and me. He put up a tent and asked me to go with him, but I refused; and he became angry and did everything he could to injure me. That man treated me most shamefully; if it had not been for Pritchard I do not know what would have become of me. Pritchard was kinder than any of the others.

After I had been a prisoner three days, Blondin came and asked me if I could ride horse back, and I said "yes," and he said if I would go with him, he would go and take two of the best horses that Big Bear had and desert that night. I told him I would *never* leave Pritchard's tent until we all left, saying "I would go and drown myself in the river before I would go with him."

Late that same night a French Canadian by the name of Pierre came into the tent, and hid himself behind us, he said the Indians wanted to shoot him, and some one told him to go and hide himself, ultimately one of the half-breeds gave a horse to save his life. Mrs. Pritchard told him not to stay in there. She did not want to see any more men killed, and one of the half-breeds took him away and he was placed under the protection of the Wood Crees. This man had been working with Goulet and Nault all winter getting out logs about thirty miles from Frog Lake.

EIGHT

Protected By Half-Breeds

*O*n the 3rd of April Big Bear came into our tent and sitting down beside us told us he was very sorry for what had happened, and cried over it, saying he knew he had so many bad men but had no control over them. He came very often to our tent telling us to "eat and sleep plenty, they would not treat us like the white man. The white man when he make prisoner of Indian, he starve him and cut his hair off." He told us he would protect us if the police came. The same day Big Bear's braves paid our tent another visit, they came in and around us with their guns, knives and tomahawks, looking at us so wickedly.

Pritchard said, "For God sake let these poor women live, they can do no harm to you; let them go home to their friends."

The leaders held a brief consultation.

An Indian stood up and pointing to the heavens said, "We promise by God that we will not hurt these white women; we will let them live."

They then left the tent.

Every time I saw one of Big Bear's Indians coming in, I expected it was to kill us, or take us away from the tent, which would have been *far worse* than death to *me*.

But they did not keep their word.

On the third night (Saturday, the 4th April,) after our captivity, two Indians came in while all the men and Mrs. Delaney were asleep, I heard them, and thought it was Pritchard fixing the harness, he usually sat up to protect us. A match was lighted and I saw two of the most hedious [*sic*] looking Indians looking over and saying where is the *Monias* squaw, meaning the white women. I got so frightened I could not move, but Mrs. Delaney put out her foot and awakened Mrs. Pritchard, and she wakened her husband, and he started up and asked what they wanted, and they said they wanted to take the white women to their tent, and I told Pritchard they could kill me before I would go, and I prayed to God to help me. Pritchard and Adolphus Nolin gave their blankets and dishes and Mrs. Pritchard, took the best blanket off her bed to give to them and they went off, and in the morning the Wood Crees came in and asked if those Indians took much from us, and Pritchard told them "No"; the Indians wanted to make them give them back. After that Pritchard and other half-breeds protected us from night to night for we were not safe a single minute.

During the two days which had passed, the bodies of the men that were murdered had not been buried. They were lying on the road exposed to the view of everyone. The half-breeds carried them off the road to the side, but the Indians coming along dragged them out again. It was dreadful to see the bodies of our *poor dear* husbands dragged back and forth by those demoniac savages.

On Saturday the day before Easter, we induced some half-breeds to take our husbands' bodies and bury them, They placed them, with those of the priests, under the church. The Indians would not allow the other bodies to be moved. And dreadful to relate those inhuman wretches set fire to the church, and with yelling and dancing witnessed it burn to the ground. The bodies, I afterwards heard, were charred beyond recognition.

Upon seeing what was done the tears ran profusely down our cheeks and I thought my very heart would break. All the comfort we received from that unfeeling band was, "that's right, cry plenty, we have killed your husbands and we will soon have you."

On Easter Sunday night there was a heavy thunder storm and before morning it turned cold and snowed; the tent pole broke, coming down within an inch of my head, the snow blowing in and our bedding all covered with it and nothing to keep us warm. I got up in the morning and found my shoes all wet and frozen, and the Indians came in and told us what they saw in the heavens. They saw a church and a man on a large black horse with his arm out and he looked so angry, and they said God must be angry with them for doing such a thing; the half-breeds are as superstitious as the Indians.

NINE

They Take Fort Pitt

The morning of the 6th of April was a memorable one. Something unusual was going to take place from the excited state of the camp. Everyone was on the go. I was in a short time made acquainted with the reason. It was more blood, more butchery, and more treachery. And oh! such a sight presented itself to my eyes. The Indians were all attired in full war habiliments. They had removed their clothes. A girdle around their waists, was all — and their paint — every shade and color. Heads with feathers, and those who had killed a white, with quills. A quill for every man scalped. Eyes painted like stars, in red, yellow and green; faces, arms, legs and bodies elaborately decorated, and frescoed in all their savage beauty, with bars, spots, rings and dots. Brandishing tomahawks, bludgeons and guns; flinging and firing them in every direction, accompanied with yells and whoops; a most hideous and terrible sight. They embraced their wives and children, and the command was given to start for Fort Pitt. In order to swell their numbers they compelled the half-breeds and some of their squaws to accompany them. The squaws ride horses like the men.

On Sunday the 12th of April they returned from the Fort flush with victory. They had captured that place, killed policeman Cowan, taken the whites prisoners, and allowed the police to escape down the river, all without loosing [*sic*] an Indian or half-breed. The prisoners were brought in while we were at dinner. Mr. and Mrs. Quinney came to our tent. Mrs. Quinney said she was cold and wet. She sat down and put her arms around me and cried. I gave her a cup of hot tea and something to eat. Shortly after the McLean's and Mann's came in. It was a great relief to see white people again.

It was not long before they moved camp about two miles from Frog Lake. Mrs. Delaney and I, walking with Mrs. Pritchard and family, through mud and water: my shoes were very thin, and my feet very wet and sore from walking. The Indians were riding beside us with our horses and buckboards, laughing and jeering at us with umbrellas over their heads and buffalo overcoats on. We would laugh and make them believe we were enjoying it, and my heart ready to break with grief all the time, When we camped, it was in a circle. A space in the centre being kept for dancing.

I asked Blondin if he had any of our stockings or underclothing in his sacks. I told me *no*, and shortly afterwards took out a pair of my husband's long stockings and put them on before me, he would change them three and four times a week. He had

A War Dance Near Fort Pitt

nearly all my poor husband's clothes. Two men came in one time while Blondin was asleep and took one of my husband's coats out of his sack and went out; Blondin upon missing it got very angry and swore before me, saying that some person had come in and taken one of his coats, and all the time I knew whose coat it was they were quarrelling over. I wished then I could close my eyes and go home to God. I went outside the tent and saw this other half-breed named Gregory Donaire with my husband's coat on and pants, and just as I looked up I thought it must be my own husband, and to see the fellow laugh in my face, he evidently had an idea about what I was thinking. Blondin wore my husband's overcoat, and all I had was my little shawl and nothing to wear on my head, and the rain pouring down in torrents on me; this fellow would walk beside the waggon and laugh, and when it quit raining asked me if I wanted *his* overcoat; I told him *no,* I did not mind being wet as much as he did. That night Mrs. Delaney and I lay down in one corner of the tent until morning came and then we had all the baking to do. We dug a hole in the ground and started a fire, taking flour, we stirred in water, kneading it hard. We then with our hands flattened it out and placed it in a frying pan, baking it before the fire, and by the time it was baked it was as black as the pan itself. We dined on bannock and bacon for two months, and were very thankful to get it.

TEN

Cooking for a Large Family

$\mathcal{M}$y experience of camp life was of such a character, that I would rather be a maid-of-all-work in any position than slush in an Indian tepee, reeking as it is, with filth and poisonous odors. There is no such a thing as an health officer among that band of braves. They have a half spiritualized personage whom they desiginate [*sic*] the Medicine Man; but he is nothing more or less than a quack of the worst kind. As in every other part of their life, so in the domestic they were unclean.

One evening, just as we had everything ready for our meal, in rushed the Big Bear's, gobbling up everything. After they had gone, I set to work to wash the dishes. Mrs. Pritchard thereat became quite angry, and would not allow me, saying that we would be glad to do more than that for the Indians yet. I went without my supper that night; I would rather starve than eat after that dirty horde.

One day, Pritchard brought in a rabbit for dinner. I thought we were going to have a treat as well as a good meal; we were engaged at other work that day, and Mrs. Pritchard did the cooking herself, but I had occasion to go in the direction of the fire, and there was the rabbit in the pot boiling, it was all there, head, eyes, feet, and everything together. My good dinner vanished there and then. I told Mrs. Delaney there was no rabbit for me. I only ate to keep myself alive and well, for if I showed signs of sickness I would have been put with the Indians, and they would have put an end to me in a short time.

We had fifteen in our tent to bake for, besides the Indians, that came in to gorge, about thirty at a time. We cut wood and carried water and did Mrs. Pritchard [*sic*] sewing for her nine children; making their clothing that came from our own house. She took some muslin that Mrs. Delaney had bought before the trouble, and cut it up into aprons for her little baby, and gave me to make, and then she went to the trunk that had all my lace trimming that I had made through the winter, and brought some for me to sew on the aprons. I made them up as neatly as I possibly could, and when finished, she thanked me for it. The little children played with keepsakes that my *mother* had given to me when a little girl, and I had to look and see them broken in pieces without a murmur, also see my friends [*sic*] photographs thrown around and destroyed. I gathered up a few that were scattered around in the dirt and saved them when no one was looking.

If Big Bear's braves would say move camp immediately, and if we should be eating and our tent not taken down just then, they would shout in the air and come and tear it down. In travelling, the Indians ride, and their squaws walk and do all the work, and they pack their dogs and have "travores" [*sic*] on their horses, upon which they tied their little children, and then all would move off together; dogs howling, and babies crying, and Indians beating their wives, and carts tumbling over the banks of the trail, and children falling, and horses and oxen getting mired down in the mud, and squaws cutting sacks of flour open to get a piece of cotton for string, and leaving the flour and throwing away the provisions, while others would come along, and gather it up. We rode on a lumber waggon, with an ox team, and some of the squaws thought we did not work enough. Not work enough, after walking or working all day, after dark we were required to bake bannock and do anything else they had a mind to give us. They wanted to work us to death.

ELEVEN

Incidents by the Way

$\mathcal{T}$he Indians are not only vicious, treacherous and superstitious, but they are childlike and simple, as the following incident will show: — After the Indians came back from Fort Pitt, one of them found a glass eye; that eye was the favorite optic of Stanley Simpson, who was taken a prisoner there by Big Bear. He brought it with him for one of his brother Indians who was blind in one eye, imagining with untutored wisdom that if it gave light to a white man, it should also to a red, and they worked at it for a time, but they could not get the focus, finally they threw it away, saying it was no good, he could not see.

While we were in camp, Mr. Quinn's little two year old girl would come in and put her little arms around our necks and kiss us. The dear little thing had no one to care for her, she would stay with us until her mother would come and take her away. The squaws also carried her around on their backs with nothing but a thin print dress on and in her bare feet. How I did feel for her, she was such a bright little girl, her father when alive took care of her. It was very hard to see her going around like any of the Indian children.

One day while travelling we came to a large creek and had to get off the waggon and pull our shoes and stockings off in order that they would be dry to put on after we got across; the water was up to our waists and we waded through. Miss McLean took her little three year old sister on her back and carried her over. After crossing we had to walk a long distance on the burnt prairie to get to the waggon, then we sat down and put our shoes on. Some of the Indians coming along said, "oh! see the monais squaw." We would laugh, tell them it was nice; that we enjoyed it. If they thought we did not, we were in danger of being taken away by them and made to work for them like their squaws.

One of Big Bear's son's wives died, and they dug a hole in the ground and wrapped blankets around her, and laid her in it, and put sacks of bacon and flour on top so that she could not get out, they covered her over with earth; and watched the place for some time for fear she would come to life again.

Their dances occur every day, they go and pick out the largest tents and go and take them from the Wood Crees, and leave them all day without any covering, with the white people who were prisoners, with them. They thought the white people took it as

- 25 -

an honor to them, and every time in moving, Big Bear's band would tell us just where to put our tents, and if one camped outside this circle, they would go and cut their tent in pieces. In some of their dances Little Poplar was arrayed in some of Miss McLean's ribbons, ties and shawls, another with my hat on, and another with Mrs. Delaney's, and the squaws with our dresses, and they had a large dish of meat in the centre and danced awhile, and sat down and ate and danced again, keeping this up all day long. And if anyone lagged in the dance, it was a bad day for him. Little Poplar had a whip, and he would ply it thick on the back of the sluggish dancer.

One day just as we were eating dinner, an Indian came and invited us out to a dog feast; the men went, but we preferred bannock and bacon, to dog. They sent each of us *three yards* of print to make us a dress; a squaw takes no more than that. And then a friendly Indian made me a present of a pair of green glasses.

A most dreadful affair occurred one day, they killed one of their squaws, an old grey headed woman that was insane. The Indians and half-breeds were afraid of her, and she told them if they did not kill her before the sun went down, she would eat the whole camp up. They got some of the half-breeds to tie her, and they carried her out on a hill, and one old half-breed struck her on the head, and the Indians shot her in the head three times, cut it off and set fire to it; they were very much afraid she would come back and do some harm to them.

One evening after making our bed for the night, four squaws came into our tent and sat down for two hours, crying and singing and clapping their hands, and after going out, some of the Indians took and tied them until morning; it was a most strange procedure. I could go on enumerating incident after incident, but I have, I think, given sufficient to give the reader an insight into their character.

TWELVE

Dancing Parties

*W*hile we were on the way too [*sic*] Fort Pitt, a letter was received from the Rev. John McDougall, of Calgary, stating that troops were coming through from Edmonton, and that they would make short work of Big Bear's band for the murders they had committed at Frog Lake. They were terribly frightened at that news, and took turns and watched on the hills night and day. Others spent their time in dancing — it was dancing all the time — all day and all night.

I will explain their mode of dancing as well as I can: — They all get in a circle, while two sit down outside and play the tom-tom, a most unmelodious instrument, something like a tambourine, only not half so *sweet*; it is made in this way: — they take a hoop or the lid of a butter firkin, and cover one side with a very thin skin, while the other has strings fastened across from side to side, and upon this they pound with sticks with all their might, making a most unearthly racket. The whole being a fit emblem of what is going on in the other world of unclean spirits. Those forming the circle, kept going around shouting and kicking, with all the actions and paraphernalia of a clown in a pantomime, only not so dumb.

We passed a short distance from where Mrs. Delaney lived, and all we could see standing, was the bell of the Catholic Mission, and when we came to Onion Lake, they had burnt some of the buildings there, and as we passed they set fire to the rest. They burnt all the flour and potatoes, some three hundred sacks, and when we reached Fort Pitt our provisions were getting scarce, and the half-breeds went to the Fort to get some flour, but the Indians had previously poured coal and machine oil on what was left, and they only got a few sacks and not very clean at that. Still we felt very thankful to have it as it was.

While in this neighbourhood, Blondin and Henry Quinn went down to the river to make their escape, and Blondin well knew that the Indians had said if one prisoner ran away they would kill all the rest. The half-breeds hearing what they had done, went after them and brought them back, and that night Big Bear's braves came into our tent where Quinn and Blondin were, and wanted to go to work and cut Quinn in pieces. Blondin was like one of themselves. Pritchard sat on his knees in front of Quinn and kept them from doing it. They were in our tent nearly the whole night with their guns, large sharp knives and war clubs. After Pritchard had talked some hours to them they went out only partly pacified. Some of them said, "he has ran [*sic*] away once, let us kill him and have no more trouble with him; if he runs away he will be going away and telling the police to come."

When near the Fort they had their "Thirst Dance." An Indian went to the bush and broke off a green bough, and carried it to the place arranged for the dance, and all the other Indians shot at it. Then the Indians got their squaws with them on horse-back; some thought it would not be polite if they did not invite the white women to help them also, and Mrs. Pritchard and another squaw came in and put Mrs. Delaney in one corner and covered her over, and me in another with a feather bed over me, so as not to find us. Then some said "Oh, let the white women stay where they are," and they took their squaws and went to the woods. I should say about fifty rode to the woods for one stick at a time, fastening a chain around it, dragged it along to this place singing and yelling as they went. After they had enough sticks, they arranged a tent in the centre of the circle. They stood a long pole up, and on this pole they tied everything they wished to give to the *sun,* and this is never taken down, and then they erected smaller poles about five feet high, all around in a large circle, and from the top of these they fastened sticks to the long pole in the centre, and covered it all with green boughs, they then partitioned the tent into small stalls, and tied print and anything bright all around inside on these poles; after they had this arranged they began dancing. It continues three days and three nights, neither eating or drinking during the entertainment. They danced all that night and the squaws had each a small whistle made of bone which they blow all the time in addition to the musical "tom-toms." Mrs. Delaney and I lay awake all night, and I said to her, "I hope the police will come in while they are having this dance." Mrs. Pritchard asked us next morning if we would go and see them at it, and remarked "they will not like it if you white women do not go and see them." We went with her, and when we got inside they laughed and were delighted at seeing us come. There they were, some of the squaws with my clothes on, and one Indian with my husband's on, and my table linen hanging on the poles. The squaws stood in those little stalls and danced. They had their faces painted, and fingers and ears filled with brass rings and thimbles. Some of the Indians were dressed in the police uniforms and had veils over their faces; and just as we got nicely there, two Indians came riding around and saying the police were all on this side of the river with their tents pitched. There must be hundreds of them, some said, and the others said *no,* because they have their wives and children with them; and then came the scattering, they ran in all directions like scared rabbits and tore their tents down, the Indians riding around on horse-back singing and yelling, and saying "let us go and meet them" that was to fight, and others said "*no,* let us move," and we all left and moved through the woods.

But it proved to be more than a mere scare. *Our* friends were drawing near — too near to to [sic] be comfortable for the *noble* "red man," the murderers of defenceless settlers, the despoilers of happy homes, the polluters of poor women and children. They did all that, and yet they are called the noble "red man." It might sound musical in the ears of the poet to write of the virtues of that race, but I consider it a perversion of the real facts. During the time I was with them I could not see anything noble in them, unless it was that they were *noble* murderers, *noble* cowards, *noble* thieves. The facts, I think, also go to show that the Indians are not treated properly. There is no distinction made between the good (there are good Indians) and bad. The character of the Indian is not studied sufficiently, or only so far as self-interest and selfish motives are concerned. But the majority of the present race can be designated anything but the noble "red man."

They would in many instances, be better without the missionary. If all denominations would only amalgamate their forces and agree upon an unsectarian basis for missionary effort, the Indians would become evangelized more quickly then they are at present. It would be better for the Indians, and more honorable for the Christian Church. Give the Indians the Gospel in its simplicity without the ritual of the denominations.

THIRTEEN

Another Battle

$\mathcal{W}$as it the distant roar of heaven's artillery that caught my ear. I listened and heard it again. The Indians heard it and were frightened.

A half-breed in a stage whisper cried, "a cannon! a cannon!"

An Indian answered, "a cannon is no good to fight."

I looked at them and it showed them to be a startled and fear-stricken company, notwithstanding that they held the cannon with such disdain as to say "cannon no good to fight." That night was full of excitement for the Indians; they felt that the enemy was drawing near, too close in fact to be safe. The prisoners were excited with the thought, that perhaps there was liberty behind that cannon for them, and taking it all round, there was little sleep within the tepees.

The next morning I awoke early with hopefulness rising within my breast at the thought of again obtaining my liberty. The first sound I heard was the firing of cannon near at hand; it sounded beautiful; it was sweet music to my ears. Anticipating the prospect of seeing friends once more, I listened and breathed in the echo after every bomb.

The fighting commenced at seven o'clock by Gen. Strange's troops forcing the Indians to make a stand. It was continued until ten with indifferent success. The troops surely could not have known the demoralized condition of the Indians, else they would have compelled them to surrender. The fighting was very near, for the bullets were whizzing around all the time. We thought surely that liberty was not far away. The Indians were continually riding back and fro inspiring their followers in the rear with hope, and we poor prisoners with despair. At last they came back and said that they had killed twenty policemen and not an Indian hurt. But there were two Indians killed, one of whom was the Worm, he who killed my poor husband, and several wounded. We were kept running and walking about all that morning with their squaws, keeping out of the way of their enemies, and our friends. We were taken through mud and water until my feet got so very sore that I could hardly walk at all.

The Indians ordered us to dig pits for our protection. Pritchard and Blondin dug a large one about five feet deep for us, and they piled flour sacks around it as a further protection; but they dug it too deep and there was two or three inches of water at the bottom. They then threw down some brush and we got into it, twenty persons in all, with one blanket for Mrs. Delaney and me. McLean's family had another pit, and his daughters cut down trees to place around it. Mr. Mann and family dug a hole in the side of the hill and crawled into it. If I had my way I would have kept out of the pit altogether and watched my chance to escape.

We fully expected the troops to follow but they did not; and early in the morning we were up and off again. Some of the Indians went back to see how about the troops, and came back with the report that the "police" (they call all soldiers police) had vanished, they were afraid. When I heard, it, I fairly sank, and the slight spark of hope I had, had almost gone out. Just to think that succor was so near, yet alas! so far. But for Mrs. Delaney I would have given way and allowed myself to perish.

General Strange

FOURTEEN

Indian Boys

*J*ust here a word about Indian boys would not be amiss. An Indian boy is a live, wild, and untamed being. He is full of mischief and cruelty to those he hates, and passably kind to those he likes. I never saw in their character anything that could be called love. They have no idea of such a tender tie. Thus by nature he is cruel without having a sense of humor, much less gayety, and in all my experience I never saw or heard one give a hearty laugh, except on the occasion of a mishap or accident to any one, and then the little fragment of humor is aroused.

He is skillful in drawing his bow and sling, and has a keenness of sight and hearing. He takes to the life of a hunter as a duck takes to water, and his delight is in shooting fowl and animals. He does it all with an ease and grace that is most astonishing. In everything of that nature he is very skillful. Pony riding is his great delight, when the ponies were not otherwise engaged, but during my stay with them, there was too much excitement and change all around for the boys to exercise that animal.

While we were driving along after breaking up camp the little fellows would run along and pick flowers for us, one vieing with the other as to who would get the most and the prettiest. They were gifted with a most remarkable memory and a slight was not very soon forgotten, while a kindness held the same place in their memory.

The general behaviour of Indian boys was nevertheless most intolerable to us white people. In the tepee there was no light and very often no fuel, and owing to the forced marches there was not much time for cutting wood, also it was hard to light as it was so green and sappy. The boys would then wrap themselves up in a blanket, but not to sleep, only to yell and sing as if to keep in the heat. They would keep this up until they finally dozed off; very often that would be in the early hours of the morning.

Like father, like son; the virtues of young Indians were extremely few. They reach their tether when they fail to benefit self. Their morality was in a very low state. I do not remember that I saw much of it, if I did it was hardly noticible [*sic*].

Where the charm of a savage life comes in I do not know, I failed to observe it during my experience in the camp of the Crees. The charm is a delusion, except perhaps when viewed from the deck of a steamer as it glided along the large rivers and lakes of the Indian country, or perhaps within the pages of a blood and thunder novel.

FIFTEEN

Hope Almost Deferred

Almost a week afterwards, on a Saturday night, the fighting Indians gathered around a tepee near ours and began that never ending dancing and singing. It was a most unusual thing for them to dance so close to our tent. They had never done so before. It betokened no good on their part and looked extremely suspicious. It seemed to me that they were there to fulfil the threat they made some time previous, that they would put an end to us soon. The hour was late and that made it all the more certain that our doom had come. I became very nervous and frightened at what was going on. When all at once there was a scattering, and running, and yelling at the top of their voices, looking for squaws and children, and tearing down tents, while we two sat in ours in the depths of despair, waiting for further developments. I clung to Mrs. Delaney like my own mother, not knowing what to do. The cause of the stampede we were told was that they had heard the report of a gun. That report was fortunate for us, as it was the intention of the Indians to wrench us from our half-breed protectors and kill us.

The tents were all down and in a very few minutes we were on the move again. It was Sunday morning at an early hour, raining heavily, and cold. We were compelled to travel all that day until eleven o'clock at night. The halt was only given then, because the brutes were tired themselves. Tents were pitched and comparative quietness reigned. Our bedding consisted of one blanket which was soaked with water. Andre Nault took pity on us and gave us his, and tried in every way to make us comfortable. I had a great aversion to that fellow; I was afraid to look at him. I was so weak and tired that I could not sleep but for only a few minutes. I had given up and despair had entered my mind. I told Mrs. Delaney I wished I could never see morning, as I had nothing to look forward to but certain death. In that frame of mind I passed the night.

SIXTEEN

Out of Big Bear's Camp

$\mathcal{M}$onday morning, May 31st, was ushered in dark and gloomy, foggy and raining, but it proved to be the happiest day we had spent since the 31st of March. As the night was passing, I felt its oppressiveness, I shuddered with the thought of what another day might bring forth; but deliverance it seems was not far away; it was even now at hand. When the light of day had swallowed up the blackness of darkness, the first words that greeted my ears was Pritchard saying "I am going to watch my chance and get out of the camp of Big Bear." Oh! what we suffered, Oh! what we endured, during those two long months, as captives among a horde of semi-barbarians. And to think that we would elude them, just when I was giving up in despair. It is said that the darkest hour is that which preceedes [*sic*] dawn; weeping may endure for a night, but joy cometh in the morning. So with me, in my utter prostration, in the act of giving way, God heard my prayer, and opened a way of deliverance, and we made the best of the opportunity.

> *"No foe, no dangerous path we lead,*
> *Brook no delay, but onward speed."*

Some of the Indians it seems had come across General Strange's scouts the night before, and in consequence, all kinds of rumors were afloat among the band. They were all very much frightened, for it looked as if they were about to be surrounded. So a move, and a quick one, was made by them, at an early hour, leaving the half-breeds to follow on. This was now the golden opportunity, and Pritchard grasped it, and with him, five other half-breed families fled in an opposite direction, thereby severing our connection with the band nominally led by Big Bear.

We cut through the woods, making a road, dividing the thick brush, driving across creeks and over logs. On we sped. At one time hanging on by a corner of the bedding in order to keep from falling off the waggon. Another time I fell off the waggon while fording a stream; my back got so sore that I could not walk much. On we went roaming through the forest, not knowing where we were going, until the night of June 3rd the cry was made by Mrs. Pritchard with unfeigned disgust, "that the police were coming." Mrs. Delaney was making bannock for the next morning's meal, while I with cotton and crochet needle was making trimming for the dresses of Mrs. Pritchard's nine half-breed babies.

I threw the trimming work to the other end of the tent, and Mrs. Delaney called upon Mrs. Pritchard to finish making the bannocks herself, and we both rushed out just as the scouts galloped in.

SEVENTEEN

Rescued

$\mathcal{R}$escued! at last, and from a life worse than death. I was so overjoyed that I sat down and cried. The rescuing party were members of General Strange's scouts, led by two friends of my late husband, William McKay and Peter Balentyne of Battleford. We were so glad to see them. They had provisions with them, and they asked us if we wanted anything to eat. We told them we had bannock and bacon, but partook of their canned beef and hard tack. It was clean and good; and was the first meal we enjoyed for two months.

I could not realize that I was safe until I reached Fort Pitt. The soldiers came out to welcome us back to life. The stories they heard about us were so terrible, that they could scarcely believe we were the same.

The steamer was in waiting to take us to Battleford. Rev. Mr. Gordon took my arm and led me on board. The same gentleman gave us hats, we had no covering for our heads for the entire two months we were captives. We were very scant for clothing. Mrs. Delaney had a ragged print dress, while I managed to save one an Indian boy brought me while in camp. Upon reaching Battleford we were taken to the residence of Mr. Laurie.

Coming down on the steamer, on nearing a little island, we saw a number of squaws fishing and waving white flags. All along wherever we passed the Indians, they were carrying white flags as a token that they had washed off their war paint and desired rest.

EIGHTEEN

We Leave For Home

$\mathcal{W}$e leave Battleford for Swift Current, and our journey takes us across the prairie; that same stretch that I travelled a few months before, but under different circumstances and associations. Then I went up as a happy bride. Now I go down *alone* and bowed with grief. Everything around is full of life, the prairie is a sea of green interpersed [*sic*] with beautiful flowers and plants. It is a pretty scene to feast upon, yet my soul cannot drink it in. I am on the way to friends, a feeling of desolation takes hold of me; but I must control myself, and by God's help I will, for his goodness is forever sure.

Rev. John McDougall, Dr. Hooper, Captain Dillon, Capt. Nash and Messrs. Fox and Bayley, of Toronto, and Mrs. Laurie accompanied us on the journey, and did everything they could to make us comfortable. The trip over the prairie was a pleasant one. When we got to the South Saskatchewan, a thunder storm came on which roughened the water so, we could not cross for about an hour. After it quieted down a scow came and carried us over. Friends there took care of us for the night, and on the 1st of July we boarded a train for Moose Jaw. Capt. Dillon on going to the post office met several young ladies in a carriage who asked where we were as they wished to take us to their homes for tea, he informed them that the train had only a few minutes to stop and that it would be impossible. Those same young ladies were back to the train before it started with a bottle of milk and a box full of eatables. At eleven o'clock p.m., we arrived at Regina, and remained with Mr. and Mrs. Fowler, going next morning to a hotel. We were there four days. At Moose Jaw we received the following kind letter from Mrs. C.F. Bennett, of Winnipeg:—

NEW DOUGLASS HOUSE, WINNIPEG, JUNE 8TH, 1885.

Mrs. Delaney and Mrs. Gowanlock:

DEAR MADAMS,— Although an entire stranger to both of you, I cannot resist the impulse to write you a few lines to say how thankful and delightful I am to hear of your rescue.

Before I was dressed this morning, my husband came up to tell me that you were both safe. And I cannot express to you, neither can you comprehend the joy that intelligence brought to *everyone.* The terrible stories of your being tortured and finally murdered, outraged the feelings of the whole civilized world, and while men swore to avenge your wrongs, women mourned you, as sisters.

I am very thankful to see by the papers that you were not so inhumanly treated as reported, although your experience has been a terrible one — and one which you can never forget.

I presume that as soon as you are a little rested, you will go east to your friends; should you do so, I will be most happy to entertain you while you are in Winnipeg.

After your captivity, you must be destitute of everything, and if you will come down here, we will be delighted to supply you with what you require. I do not know if you have personal friends here, or not, but your sufferings have given you a sister's place in every heart, and *every one* in Winnipeg would be deeply disappointed if you did not give them an opportunity of expressing their deep sympathy and regards.

Mr. Bennett unites with me in best wishes, and in hopes that you will accept our hospitality on your way east.

I am in deepest sympathy,

Sincerly yours,

MRS. C.F. BENNETT.

I shall never forget the words of sympathy that are expressed in this epistle, or the kindness of Mr. and Mrs. McCaul and the people of Winnipeg generally. On our way from Winnipeg to Parkdale we received every attention and assistance, which I can assure the reader went a long way in making sorrow lighter and more able to bear. I thank God for the sympathy that was extended to me by his people. Mr. J.K. Macdonald of Toronto, was most assiduous in his attention to us from Winnipeg until we left the train at Parkdale on the 12th of July. I must not forget the kindness of Mr. and Mrs. Armstrong also of Toronto, or the other ladies and gentlemen who were our fellow-passengers on the journey.

NINETEEN

At Home

$\mathcal{H}$ome — torn from mine — back to the parental. I will now look back over the scene, taking a panoramic view of the whole, as it occurred from the day I left my father's house full of happiness and joy, until I entered it full of sorrow and suffering.

It is well for mankind that they are forbidden the knowledge of what will be their destiny. It was well-conceived by a loving father that it was for our interest to be kept in ignorance of what was in store, for we, his creatures. And thus it was that I entered upon the duties of the household, with a lightness of heart equal to that of any matron. In the humble home (I commence from there) in that beautiful north-west land of quietness and peace, there was not a ruffle heard, or a rumor sounded, of what was in store for that industrious little community. We were living in the bonds of fellowship with all mankind, and we had no fear. But in all that stillness there was an undercurrent at work that would soon make itself felt. Dissatisfaction on account of grievances, real or fancied, was blowing. It had broken out in one place, why should it not in another. This disaffected spirit was prevalent in all parts of that country. Who was to blame? who was the cause? direct or indirect, it is not my intention or desire to say: suffice it is to note, that there was discontent; and therefore there must have been grievances, and an attempt should have been made or an understanding arrived at, whereby this state of discontent should have been replaced by that of content, without disturbance. Where there is discontent there must be badness and suffering, with evils and excesses lying in its wake.

To have removed those grievances was the imperative duty of the dispensers of law and order and thus avoid those excesses, but it was not done in time and the inevitable did come swift and sure; the innocent were made to feel its fury. For that little hamlet by the creek was entered, and its domestic quietness destroyed and future prospects blighted. There was a degree of uneasiness felt after we were informed of the horror of Duck Lake. Two halfbreeds, Blondin and Donaire, who were employed by my husband, were observed in frequent and earnest conversation with the Indians. Those two had but arrived from the scene at Duck Lake. For what were they there? Was it to incite the Indians? Their actions were, to say the least, suspicious.

I will not dwell on the terrible slaughter which followed, it is too painful a subject, simply stating that I had not believed that anything so awful would have been perpetrated by either half-breeds or Indians, until we were taken out of Mrs.

Delaney's the second time, and then I felt that there would be trouble, but not in such a manner as that. When I was dragged from the death-bed of my husband, who had the ground for a couch and the canopy of heaven for a coverlet, I was in a bewildered condition. Half-unconsciously I allowed the Indian to drag me on to his tepee, and once in, the circumstances which led to my position, flitted through my brain in quick succession. I then realized that it was most critical; in a few hours I would be forced to undergo ill-treatment that would very soon kill me. With those thoughts within my mind, the tepee opened and a little girl entered, an angel sent by God to be my deliverer. Although not aware, she was his instrument in taking me out of danger and placing me in a purer atmosphere. That child was Pritchard's little girl and I asked her to send her father. He came and by his influence I was transferred to his care for a while. And when I entered his tent and there saw Mrs. Delaney, I was overjoyed for a minute, and then all was a blank; the excitement proved too much for me and I swooned away. When I returned to consciousness they were all doing their best for me.

In a short time Blondin came in, (at the commencement of the massacre he left for our house) he brought with him our waggon, and oxen, and all the furniture and provisions he could take. Immediately thereafter the Indians appeared and it was then that he offered them $30 and a horse for our release. The offer was accepted and I was transferred to Blondin. The wretch was there with evil intent in his heart. I fully believe that he felt exultant over the doings of the day. Why did he go down to our house when that dreadful affair was going on? Why did he help himself to our goods? *Only* for a bad purpose. Oh! God I saw it all. He had everything arranged for me to live with him. All my husband's things; all my things; and a tent. But I refused to accept him or his conditions. I resented the infamous proposals as strongly as I was able, and appealed to John Pritchard for protection and he generously granted my request. I will never forget his kindness to me as long as I live: " Yes, Mrs. Gowanlock, you can share my tent, with myself and family, and I will protect you."

That dated the commencement of the shameful treatment I received at the hands of Blondin, and whenever Pritchard was absent, it was meted out to me to the full. Blondin purchased my liberty, that would have been a good action if prompted by honorable motives, but in the absence of that it has no weight with me. He was amply repaid, he got our oxen, our waggon, our provisions, our clothes, we had money there, perhaps he got that. I have wondered since was it not my money with which he purchased me. By the help of God I was saved from him; and a life worse than death. If the worst had come I would have drowned or killed myself; but it did not. "God moves in a mysterious way."

During the next two months I was called upon to witness heart-rending scenes; first the brutal treatment of the dead bodies of our husbands', as well as cruelty to ourselves; for even under Pritchard's care we were not safe and did not know what minute would be our last. Not content with murdering them in cold blood, they must needs perform diabolical deeds which causes me to shudder when I think of it. They danced around them with demoniac glee, kicking and pulling them in every direction, and we were the unwilling witnesses of such behaviour. And when we had them buried under the church they burned it down, with dancing and yelling, accompanied with hysterical laughter. The sight was sickening to me and I was glad they moved in the direction of Fort Pitt, leaving that place with all its associations of suffering and death. But when I heard that they intended to take the Fort, and destroy more life, I felt that I would rather remain where we were than witness any more scenes of so sad a nature. I have no happy tale to tell for this period was filled with woe and pain.

I will not enumerate further the trials I had to undergo day after day, but will pass rapidly on until the gladsome note was sounded by our hostess Mrs. Pritchard the "police are here." God delivered us again.

It is unnecessary to itemize in detail what passed from that time until I reached Ontario. I have told my tale, simple and truthful, and what remains for me now is my old home, my old associations, and my old life — the lines are hard to bear— "Thy will not mine be done."

> Once I thought my cross to heavy,
> And my heart was sore afraid,
> Summoned forth to stand a witness
> For the cause of truth betrayed.
>
> "Send, O Lord," I prayed, "some Simon,
> As of old was sent to Thee."
> "Be a Simon," said the Master,
> "For this cross belongs to me."
>
> Still is crucified my Saviour,
> I myself must a Simon be;
> Take my cross and walk humbly
> Up the slopes of Calvary.

To One of the Absent

You bade me good-bye with a smile, love,
And away to the west wild and drear;
At the sound of war's bugle shrill calling
You went without shadow of fear.
But when I complained of your going,
To face dangers untold in the west;
You chided me gently by singing:
"Encourage me dear 'twill be best."

"I know you will miss me each hour
And grieve when I'm far, far away:
But its duty's demand and I'm ready;
Could I show the white feather to-day?
Oh! Now, you're my own bright eyed blessing
And show the true spirit within:
Those eyes now so fearlessly flashing
Shall guide me through war's crash and din."

With your men you went cheerful and willing,
To defend and take peace to the poor
Helpless children and sad prisoned women
Who had homes on Saskatchewan's shore,
And now I'm so proud of you darling
I can worship a hero so brave,
While I pray for your safe home returning;
When the peace flag shall quietly wave.

O'er the land where poor Scott's heartless murderer,
Has added much more to his sin;
By the cold-blooded uncalled for slaughter,
Of Gowanlock, Delaney and Quinn,
Who like many others now sleeping,
Shroudless near the sky of the west,
May be called the sad victims and martyrs
Of Riel who's name we detest.

Many hearts are now mourning their lov'd ones
Who died at their post, true and brave,
In defiance of one heartless rebel,
Who's life not e'en "millions" should save.
So keep your arm strong for the fray dear,
I'll not wish you back 'ere the fight
Shall decide for you, country and comrades,
In favor of honour and right.

Let justice be done now unfailing
Nought but death *can atone for his sin;*
Let the fate he has meted to others;

By our dauntless be meted to him,
Don't return until quiet contentment;
Fills the homes now deserted out west,
And the true ring of peace finds an echo,
In each sturdy settler's breast.

And when you are homeward returning,
With heart that has never known fear;
Remember the love light is burning,
Unceasingly, constantly, here
And "Bright Eyes" will give you a welcome
Which even a soldier may prize
While the lips will be smiling with pleasure,
That have prayed in your absence with sighs.

And the whole world shall ring with the praises
Of Canada's noblest and best;
Who shoulder to shoulder defended,
And saved the unhappy North-West
While in coming years 'round the hearthstone
Will be told how the dark coats and red,
Put to rout Riel, rebels and half-breeds
And aveng'd both the living and dead.

CLEOMATI
20 Alexander St., Toronto.

SHOT DOWN

*T*hey died a brutal death on the 2nd of April, disarmed first, and then shot down. The perpetrators of that outrage were actuated by fiendish instincts, nevertheless they had an intuition of what was meant by civilization. How they could have so forgotten the training they had received religiously and socially to have allowed the lower instincts of the savage to gain the ascendancy and fell in cold blood — not extortioners or land-grabbers — but their spiritual advisers; their superintendent; their farm instructor, and those who had left comfortable homes in the east in order to carry civilization into the remote places of the west. The work that they were performing was calculated to elevate the Indian and make him a better man; taking him from his miserable mode of living and leading him into a more happy and prosperous life for this and the next. It is unaccountable, and there is yet a something that will come to the surface that was the real cause for this dreadful act. At this point a brief sketch of the lives of some of those killed would not be out of place.

They numbered nine, the entire male population of that growing little village. There were T. Quinn, J. Delanay [*sic*], J.A. Gowanlock, T. Dill, W.C. Gilchrist, J. Williscraft, C. Gouin and Father Fafard and a priest from Onion Lake. Mr. Quinn was the Indian agent for that district well fitted in every particular for the position he held. Mr. Dill kept a general store and at one time lived at Bracebridge, was a brother of the member of Muskoka in the local house. Mr. Williscraft came from Owen Sound where his friends reside. C. Gouin was a native of the north-west.

MR. GOWANLOCK

*J*ohn Alexander Gowanlock, one of the Frog Lake martyrs, was born in the City of Stratford, Province of Ontario, on the 17th of April, 1861. He was the youngest son of Mr. Jas. Gowanlock, of East Otto, Cattaraguas County, New York State. He has three brothers living, and one sister, A.G. and J. Gowanlock of Parkdale, Ontario, R.K. Gowanlock, of Oscoda, Michigan, and Mrs. Daisy Huntsman, of Tintern, Co. Lincoln. From a boy he was a general favorite, quiet and unassuming, yet withal, firm and decided in his opinions. After leaving Stratford he resided for some time in Barrie, and then went to the Village of Parkdale, where he resided until he left for the north-west.

Being in ill-health (at the age of 19), his physician and aunt, Dr. J.K. Trout, of Toronto, advised a change of climate, and acting upon that advice left for that great country. After a short residence every symptom of disease had vanished, and upon his return some eighteen months after, he felt and was a new man in every particular. In three months time he returned to the land of his adoption. By honesty and energy he succeeded well. He took hold of every kind of work that he thought would pay. He became farmer, mill-builder, speculator, surveyor, store- keeper and mill-owner in succession, buying and selling, and at the same time pushing further west. His greatest success was in Battleford, the Indians of that district would flock to his store, because they knew they could get a good article at a reasonable price. Last year the Government wanted mills for the reserves in the region of Frog Lake, and after negotiating with them for some time he finally decided, in conjunction with Mr. Laurie, to accept the offer made, the Government giving them the sum of $2,800 as an inducement.

Mr. Gowanlock

In the month of October of last year, he began operations, which, if those poor, deluded savages, who did not know when they were well off, had allowed him to finish, would long ere this been a hive of industry and a blessing to those Indians. He visited Ontario the same year, buying all the machinery necessary, for the mills and superintending its shipment. He also took unto himself a wife from among the fair daughters of Ontario, and never a happier couple went forth to brave the cares of life. Both young and full of energy.

But they were not allowed to enjoy their domestic bliss long. The sad event which terminated with him being murdered, along with eight others, being still fresh in the memory of all; it was a sudden call, but he was prepared for it. An oath was never uttered by him, nor did he know the taste of liquor, a temperance man in the full meaning of the term. He also took a hearty interest in church matters having been one of the managers of the Battleford Prebyterian [sic] Church. Wherever he went he did good, in a gentle and kind way; and he will be remembered by both Indian, half-breed and settler, as one who never took advantage of them in any way, and the very soul of honor.

> *Not himself, but the truth that in life he had spoken,*
> *Not himself, but the seed that in life he had sown,*
> *Shall pass to the ages — all about him forgotten,*
> *Save the truth he had spoken, the things he had done.*

MR. GILCHRIST

*O*ne of the victims of the Frog Lake massacre was William Campbell Gilchrist, a native of the village of Woodville, Ontario, and eldest son of Mr. J.C. Gilchrist, Postmaster of that place. He was an energetic young man, of good address, and if spared would have made his mark in the land of promise. Prior to going there, he held situations in various parts of this province, and they were all of such a nature, as to make him proficient in the calling of his adoption, he had splendid business ability and with a good education, made progress that was quite remarkable for one of his years, at the time of his murder he was only in his twenty-fourth year.

He was clerk for Mr. E. McTavish of Lindsay, for some time: he then returned to his home to take a situation which had been offered him by Mr. L.H. Staples, as assistant in his general store; he afterwards went to the village of Brechin as Clerk and Telegraph Operator, for Messrs. Gregg & Todd. While there he formed the acquaintance of Mr. A.G. Cavana, a Surveyor, and it was through his representations that he directed his steps to the great unknown land. Shortly after his acquaintance with Mr. Cavana, that gentleman received a government appointment as surveyor in the territories, taking Mr. Gilchrist with him in the capacity of book keeper and assistant surveyor; they left in the spring of 1882. He was well fitted for the position, for besides being an excellent penman, was an expert at figures; when the winter set in, he remained there, taking a situation in a store in Winnipeg, and when the summer opened out he again went with Mr. Cavana on the survey, (1883) on his way home in the autumn he fell in with Mr. J.A. Gowanlock, who induced him to remain with him as clerk, with whom he never met until that sad morning on the 2nd of April, when he was shot down in his strength and manhood. He was a member of the Presbyterian church having confessed at the early age of 14 years. It was his intention to enter the Manitoba College as a theological student.

Mr. Gilchrist

REV. ADELARD FAFARD

*L*eon Adelard Fafard, as the name denotes, was a French Canadian, born at St. Cuthbert, in the County of Berthier, Province of Quebec, on the 8th of June, 1850. He was a son of Mr. Charles Fafard, cultivator, St. Cuthbert, and brother of Dr. Chas. Fafard, Jr., Amherst, Montreal. He entered the College of the Assumption on September 1st, 1864. From early years, he was devoted to his religion, and an enthusiastic student. He entered a monastic life on the 28th of June, 1872, and took his first vows on the 29th of June, 1873, one year later, and his perpetual vows on June the 29th, 1874.

In the Catholic Mission No. 839, July 3rd, 1885, Monseignor Grandire says, Poor Father Fafard belonged to the Diocese of Montreal; he entered our congregation in 1872, and received his commission for my missions in 1875. I ordained him priest on December 8th, 1875, and sent him successively on missons to the savages under the direction of an experienced father. He was always distinguished for his zeal and good tact. For nearly two years he was Superior of a district, and by superhuman efforts succeeded in making a fine establishment by working himself, as a hired laborer, in order to diminish the expenses of his district.

Rev. P. Lebert speaks of him as a pious, humble, subdued, very obedient, full of good will and courage. He adds that he had talent and showed a good disposition for preaching; his voice was full and strong, and his health robust. He was beginning to see the fruits of his labors, when on the 2nd of April, 1885, he was so fouly murdered while administering consolation to dying men.

Father Fafard

- 47 -

MR. DILL

Geo. Dill who was massacred at Frog Lake, was born in the Village of Preston, in the County of Waterloo, Ont., and was at the time of his death about 38 years of age. At the age of about 17 years, he joined his brother, who was then trading for furs at Lake Nipissing, in 1864. In 1867 his brother left Nipissing, leaving him the business, which he continued for a few years, when he left that place and located on a farm on Bauchere Lake in the Upper Ottawa River. In 1872 he went to Bracebridge, Muskoka, where his brother, Mr. J.W. Dill, the present member for the Local Legislature, had taken up his residence and was doing business. After a short time, he set up business as a general store at Huntsville, where he remained until 1880; he then took a situation in a hardware store in the Village of Bracebridge. While living in Huntsville, he was married to Miss Cassleman, of that place. They had a family of two children, who are now living somewhere in Eastern Canada. In 1882, at the time of the Manitoba boom, he went to see that country, and engaged with a Doininion Land Surveyor, retiring to Bracebridge again in the winter following, remaining till spring 1883, he again went to the North-West, and again engaged with a Surveyor; his object was to secure a good location and settle down to farming, but his inclination led him to trading again, and after speculating until the fall of 1884, he left Battleford for Frog Lake.

He was the only trader in the Frog Lake district, and was well respected by the community generally.

Mr. Dill

Part 2
Being the Story
of Theresa Delaney

PREFACE

$\mathcal{S}$everal friends have asked me to write a sketch of my life and more especially of my adventures in the North-West. At first I hesitated before promising to comply with the request. There is a certain class of orators who, invariable [*sic*], commence their public address by stating that they are "unaccustomed to public speaking." It may be true in many cases, but most certainly no public speaker was ever less accustomed to address an audience, than I am to write a book. Outside my limited correspondence, I never undertook to compose a page, much less a book. But, if any excuse were necessary, I feel that the kindness of the people I have met, the friendliness of all with whom I have come in contact, during the last eventful half-year, would render such excuse uncalled for. I look upon the writing of these pages as a duty imposed upon me by gratitude. When memory recalls the sad scenes through which I have passed, the feeling may be painful, but there is a pleasure in knowing that sympathy has poured a balm upon the deep wounds, and that kindness and friendship have sweetened many a bitter drop in the cup of my sorrow and trouble.

"There is a tide in the affairs of men," sang England's great Bard, but we never know when it is about to turn, or if that turn will be the ebb or the flow of happiness. "The veil of the Future is woven by the hand of Mercy." Could I have but caught a glimpse through its folds, some three years ago, I might not have the story to tell that you, kind reader, will find in this short work. I might not be, to-day, mourning the loss of a dear husband.

But who can judge of the ways of Divine Providence? For His own wise ends has the Almighty permitted such things to take place: and submissive to His will, I feel that instead of repining, I should return Him thanks for my own life and preservation; and, under God, I must thank my friends one and all!

If this little sketch should prove instructive or even interesting to anyone I will feel doubly repaid. The scenes I have to describe, the story I have to tell, would require the pen of a Fenimore Cooper to do them justice. Feeling myself unable to relate all I experienced and suffered, in an adequate manner, I will merely offer the public, a simple, truthful, unvarnished tale and for every fact thereof, I give my word that it is no fiction, but real truth.

With this short preface I will now crave the indulgence of my readers, while they peruse the following pages.

Theresa Delaney

ONE

My Youth and Early Life

As the principal object of this work, is to give an account of my experiences in the North-West, and my many adventures during the last few months, I would deem it out of place to detain my readers with any lengthy description of my birth-place or any details of my younger days. I have noticed many false reports that have been circulated through the press, upon the different situations and conditions in the North-West — whether as to the whites, the half-breeds, or the Indians. In the second chapter I will give a truthful version of what I saw, heard and know. Still I cannot well enter upon this work, with justice to myself or to my late husband, without informing my readers whence we came and how our lots happened to be cast together amidst the scenes of our new home, and upon the theatre of the fearful tragedy in which we played such important parts.

My grandfather, Henry Marshall Fulford, while yet a young man, about the year 1812, came from Woburn Massachusetts, and established his home on the Aylmer road, near Bytown, the Ottawa of to-day, where he carried on an extensive lumbering and farming business. My father was born there, and it was also the place of my own birth. Our home was situated about two miles and a half from Aylmer, and about five miles from the present capital of the Dominion.

In those days Ottawa was called Bytown. No one then dreamed that it was destined to become the capital and the seat of the future Federal government of the country. The town, for it was then a town, was small and far from attractive, and the surrounding country was not very much inhabited. The lumbering operations constituted the stable commerce, and the shanties were the winter homes of the greater number of the people.

Nearly all my life, except the last three years, was spent at home. I never travelled much, and in fact, never expected to become a traveller, and above all, an unwilling heroine in the North-West troubles. I had several sisters and brothers. I was the eldest of the family, and as such, for many years had to devote my time to household cares. My school-days seem now the pleasantest period of my early life. Since then I have known many ups and downs; but never felt the same peace of mind and gayness of spirit that I have felt in days now gone. I might say that I have lived three distinct lives. From my birth until the day of my marriage, which took place on the 27th of July, 1882, I led a uniform life. Few, if any changes, marked each passing year. The seasons came and went, and the winter's snow fell and the summer's sun ripened the golden harvests, and days flowed into weeks, weeks into months, months into years, and year succeeded year as I felt myself growing into womanhood. The changes in my life were few and my troubles so small, that memory had scarcely ever to recall a dark or dreary scene and hope always beckoned me on to the future.

The only events that seemed to stand out, landmarks in the past, were two deaths in the family — the first my eldest brother and the second my dearly beloved and much lamented father.

Had it not been for these two events I might drop a veil over all the past and consider merely that I had lived through such a number of years: — these years, like the great desert of the east, would stretch back, an unbroken tract, with no object to break the monotony of the scene. But, as the kirches tombs or monuments of Arabia, rise up in solemn grandeur from out the lonliness [sic] of the plain, casting their shadows of the sandy waste, so these two monuments or tombs appear upon the level scene of my uneventful past. Could I, then, have caught one glimpse adown the valley of the "Yet to be," what a different picture would have presented itself to my vision! A confusion of adventures, a panorama never ending, ever shifting, of an eventful life.

My second life might be called a period from my wedding day until the 2nd of April, 1885. And the third, the last and most eventful life, is that of three months — April, May and June, 1885. To the second important period in my career I will consecrate the next chapter and to the third and final part of my life will be devoted the last chapter.

My husband was born in Napean, in the Province of Ontario, about the end of 1846. Physically speaking, he was a man of very fine appearance. Over six feet in height and weighing about two hundred and ten pounds. His youth was spent in his native place, where he went to school and where he commenced his life of labor and exertion. I don't know, exactly, when it was that I first met him; but I must have been quite young, for I remember him these many years. He was, during the last ten years that he lived in the Ottawa valley, foreman for different lumber firms. Naturally gifted to command, he knew the great duty of obedience, and this knowledge raised him in the estimation of all those whose business he undertook to direct. And owing to that good opinion, he received a general recommendation to the government, and in the year 1879, he was appointed Indian instructor for the north-west.

Like my own life, his was uneventful. Outside the circle of his friends — and that circle was large — he was unknown to the public. Nor was he one of those who ever sought notoriety. His disposition was the very opposite of a boastful one.

Often I heard tell of the north-west. But I never took any particular interest in the country previous to his appointment and departure for his new sphere. I knew by the map, that such a region existed — just as I knew that there was a Brazil in South America, or a vast desert in the centre of Africa. Our statesmen were then forming plans to build the great Pacific Road, that band of iron which was soon destined to unite ocean to ocean. However, I never dreamed that I would one day visit those vast regions, the former home of the buffalo, the haunt of the prairie-chicken and the prairie-wolf. It never dawned upon me, that as I watched the puffing of the engine that rushed along the opposite side of the Ottawa from my home, that, one day, I would go from end to end of that line, — pass over those vast plains and behold the sun set, amidst the low poplars of the rolling prairies, — listen to the snort of the same engine as it died away, in echo, amongst the gorges of the Rockies. My husband had been three years, previous to our marriage, in the north west. His first winter was spent at "Onion Lake," there being no buildings at "Frog Lake." In fact, when he arrived there, "Frog Lake" district was a wilderness. During those three years I began to take some interest in that "land of the setting sun," — but, as yet, I scarcely imagined that I would ever see the places he described. In 1882, my husband returned to Ottawa and his principal object in coming, was to take me, as his wife, away with him to his new home.

We were married in Aylmer on the 27th July, 1882. Our intention was to start for the wilds on the first day of August. In the next chapter I will take up that second period of my life and strive to describe our trip and what we saw, learned and experienced during the following three years.

My readers will have to excuse what may seem egotism on my part, in speaking so much about myself and my husband. But as the subject demands that I should detail, all that can be of any public interest, in my short life, it would be difficult to write my story and not appear, at times, somewhat egotistical.

This first chapter must necessarily be short, when one has nothing to write about it is hard to fill up pages, and my life, and that of my husband, so far as I know, were most uneventful up to the day of our union, when

> "We joined the hands of each other,
> To move through the stillness and noise
> Dividing the cares of existence,
> But doubling its hopes and its joys."

My younger days seem to have passed away like a quiet dream, leaving but a faint memory behind; but my last period of life resembles more some frightful night-mare and I often wonder can it be true that I have passed through such scenes or is the whole affair a fevered vision of the night!

Now that I am safely home again with my good dear mother beside me, my fond brothers and sisters around me, it would appear as if I had never got married, never left them, never saw the north-west, never suffered the exposure, loss, sorrow, turmoil, dangers and terrors of the late rebellion. But fancy cannot destroy the truth — the real exists in spite of the ideal, and, as I enter upon my description, faint and imperfect as it may be, I feel my hand shake with nervous excitement, my pulse throb faster, my heart beat heavier, as scene after scene of the great drama passes before me, clear and perfect as when first enacted. Had I only the language at my command, as I have the pictures before me, at my summons — I feel that I could do justice to the subject. But as I was never destined to be an authoress and my powers of composition were dealt out to me with a sparing hand, I can but express my regret that an abler writer does not hold my pen. A cloud has come over my life-dream. The angel of death passed by and in the shadow of his wing a heavy and better stroke was dealt. It may not be of much interest to the public to know how I feel over my loss, but if each one would, for a moment, suppose the case their own and then reflect upon what the feeling must be. Let them attempt to write a cold, matter-of-fact statement of the events, to detail them simply as they took place, without giving expression to sentiments of sorrow, I think that, at least, ninety-nine out of every hundred would fail, and the one who could succeed would appear, in my mind, a person without heart or feeling, unable to love and unworthy of affection.

I will strive to push on to the end of my undertaking, without tiring my readers, with vain expressions of sorrow, regret or pain; but do not expect that I can relate the story from first to last, without giving vent to my feelings.

There is one pleasure, however, in knowing that I have no complaints to make, no blame to impute, no bitter feelings to arouse, no harsh words to say. But on the contrary, I will try not to forget the kindness, sympathy, and protection, that from one source or another were tendered to me.

I hope this little book will please all who read it; amuse some; instruct others; but I pray sincerely that not one of all my readers may ever be placed in the painful situation through which I have passed. Methinks some good prayers have gone up to heaven for me, and that the Almighty lent an attentive ear to the supplications; for like the angel that walked through the flaming furnace to protect the just men of old, some spirit of good must have stood by my side to guide me in safety through the fiery ordeal and to conduct me to that long wished for haven of rest — my old home on the Aylmer Road.

TWO

My Marriage Life

$\mathcal{M}$y wedding took place in the usual manner; the same congratulations, presents, kisses, well-wishes all the world over. I need not dwell upon the event any further.

On the 1st August, 1882, my husband took the train at Ottawa, *en route* for the North-West. As far as the first portion of our trip is concerned I have little or nothing to say, I could not see much from the car window and every place was new to me and, in fact, one place seemed as important as another in my eyes.

We passed through Toronto and thence to Sarnia, and on to Chicago. We crossed to Port Huron and proceeded at once to St. Paul. This was our first stoppage. We spent a day in St. Paul, and, indeed, the city deserves a day, at least, from all who travel that way. It is a beautiful place. However, it seemed to me much on the same plan and in the same style as all the Western American cities. From St. Paul's we went on to Winnipeg. I must say that I was not very favourably impressed by my first visit to this metropolis of the North-West. On my homeward trip I found vast changes for the better in the place. Still it may have been only to my eye that the city appeared far from clean, and anything but attractive. I must admit that it was rainy weather — and oh! the mud! I have heard that there are two classes of people leave Quebec after a first visit — the one class are those who caught a first glimpse of the Rock City on a beautiful day. These people are unceasing in their admiration of Quebec. The other class are those, who came into the city, for the first time, on a rainy day, when the streets were canals and mud was ankle deep. It would be impossible to convince these people that Quebec was anything but a filthy, hilly, crooked, ugly, unhealthy place. I may be of the latter class, when I refer to Winnipeg. But most assuredly I am not prejudiced, for since my last passage through that city I have changed my idea of it completely.

From Winnipeg we proceeded by rail to Brandon and thence, by construction train, to Troy. We were then four hundred miles from Winnipeg and we had four hundred miles to travel. But our cars ceased here. At Troy we got our tent ready, supplied ourselves with the necessaries upon such a journey, and getting our buckboard into order, we started upon the last, the longest and yet pleasantest part of our voyage.

How will I attempt to describe it! There is so much to tell and yet I know not what is best to record and what is best to leave out.

Half a day's journey from Troy we crossed the Qu'Appelle river. The scenery upon the banks of that most picturesque of streams would demand the pencil of a Claude Lorraine, or the pen of a Washington Irving to do it justice. Such hills I never before beheld. Not altogether for size but for beauty. Clad in a garb of the deepest green they towered aloft, like the battlement of two rival fortresses — and while the sun lit up the hills to our right, the shades of mid-day deepened upon the frowning buttresses to our left. Every tree seemed to have a peculiar hue, a certain depth of color completely its own. Indeed, one would imagine that Dame Nature had

Mr. Delaney

been trying a gigantic crazy quilt and had flung it over the bed of the Qu'Appelle valley, that all who went by might admire her handiwork.

I might here remark that the days of the summer are longer, in the north-west, than in the Ottawa district. In fact, we used to rise at three o'clock in the morning and drive for three hours before our breakfast. It would then be grey dawn and the flush of approaching day-light could be seen over the eastern hills. At nine o'clock in the evening it would be twilight. The days of midwinter are proportionately shorter.

The road we had to travel was a lovely one; at times it might be a little rough, but indeed it could well compare with most of the roads in our more civilized places. Nearly every night we managed to reach a clump of bushes or shelter to camp. Except for two days, when on the "Salt Plains," when like the caravans in the deserts of the east we had to carry our own fuel and water.

We crossed the South Saskatchewan at Aroline — or the "Telegraph Crossing," also known as Clark's Ferry — from the man who kept the ferry, and who made the new trail running to the Touchwood Hills. We again crossed the the North Saskatchewan near Fort Pitt — which is thirty-five miles from our destination.

We went by the river road, and after we crossed the salt plains, and got into the woods at Eagle Creek, we had a splendid trip through a rich fertile abundant farming country. The houses are not very attractive, but the farms are really fine. I will dwell upon this question at a greater length presently.

That less confusion may take place, I will sub-divide this chapter into three sections. In the first I will speak of the farms and farmers — their homes and how they live; in the second, I will describe our own home and its surroundings: and in the third, I will speak of the Indians under my husband's control, and tell how we got along during the three years I was there.

The Farmers and Their Farms

It would be out of place and even impossiby [*sic*] for me, at present to give you any figures relating to the crops and harvests of the North-West. Suffice, to say that for two summers, at Frog Lake, in my husband's district, we raised wheat that was pronounced by competent judges to equal the best that ever grew in Ontario.

The land is fertile and essentially a grain-bearing soil. It is easy to clear, and is comparatively very level. There is ample opportunity to utilize miles upon miles of it, and the farms that exist, at present, are evidences of what others might be. No one can tell the number of people that there is room for in the country. Europe's millions might emigrate and spread themselves over that immense territory, and still there would be land and ample place for those of future generations. We were eight hundred miles from Winnipeg, and even at that great distance we were, to use the words of Lord Dufferin, "only in the anti-chamber of the great North-West."

The country has been well described by hundreds, it has also been falsely reported upon by thousands. At first it was the "Great Lone Land," — the country of bleak winter, eternal snow and fearful blizzards. Then it became a little better known, and, suddenly it dawned upon the world that a great country lie [*sic*] sleeping in the arms of nature, and awaiting the call of civilization to awaken it up and send it forth on a mission of importance. The "boom" began. All thoughts were directed to the land of the Rockies. Pictures of plenty and abundance floated before the vision of many thousands. Homes in the east were abandoned to rush into the wilds of the West. No gold fever of the South was ever more exciting, and to add thereto, they found that the government proposed building a line of railway, from end to end of the Dominion. Then the Frazer [*sic*], Saskatchewan, Red River and Assiniboine became household words.

In this story of a fancied land of plenty, there was much truth, but as in every case in life, there was much falsehood as well. It suited the purpose of monied speculators to laud to the skies the North-west in general. But rich and extensive as the land may be, no man can expect to make a fortune there, unless through hard labor, never ceasing exertion and great watchfulness. There, as in all other lands, you must "earn your bread by the sweat of your brow." That sentence passed on man, when the first sin darkened his soul, shall exist and be carried into execution unto the end of time. And no man is exempt, and no land is free from it. Many have failed in finding riches in the North-West; gold did not glitter along the highway, nor were precious stones to be picked up in every foot path. The reason is, because they went there expecting to have no work to do merely to sit down, to go to bed, to sleep and wake up some morning millionaires. But those who put their shoulder to the wheel and their hands to the plough, turned up as rich a soil as England's flag floats over, and sowed seeds that gave returns as plentiful as the most abundant harvests on the continent. It would do one good to drive along the river road by the Saskatchewan, and observe those elegant, level, fertile, well tilled farms that dot the country. It is a great distance to procure materials for building, and as yet the most of the houses are rough and small, but comfortable and warm, and sufficient for the needs of the farmers.

Much of the labor is done in the old style, as in my own native place, before the days of machinery. But soon we will see the mower and reaper finding their way into the very furthest settlements — and if ever there was a country laid out for the use of machinery it is certainly the north-west.

Before many years, there will be good markets for the produce, as the towns are growing up pretty rapidly and the railroad is lending a great encouragement to the farmers near the line.

Half a century ago the country was unheard of, save through the Hudson Bay Company's agents and factors: quarter of a century ago it was considered a *probably* future portion of our Dominion. Behold it to-day ! Its cities, its roads, its villages, its farms, its inhabitants! What then may the immense territory not become before fifty years more shall have rolled into eternity? I do not feel myself competent to judge — but I have no doubt but it will become the grainery of the continent and the supplier of half Europe.

The farmer in the Provinces who has a good farm and who can make a fair living would be foolish to leave it for the hazard of an attempt in the new country. But should a person be commencing life and have the intention of depending upon themselves, their own exertion and energy, then the sun shines not on a finer land, holding out a broader prospect than in that great country that lies towards the Pacific.

I have only spoken hurriedly and from a general standpoint of the farmers, and when I say farmers, I mean white people. The Indian farming is of a different nature altogether. That will demand my attention before I close this chapter.

Frog Lake and Surroundings

Although the name of the place would indicate that the lake abounded in frogs, still I have no recollection of seeing any extra number of them around the place. I think the name comes from a tradition — perhaps in some age, long lost in the twilight of Indian story, the frogs may have been more plentiful in that special locality than elsewhere. Twenty miles from our farm and twelve miles from Fort Pitt is "Onion Lake" farm, where my husband spent his first winter. I cannot tell how that place got its name no more than how our district was called *Aieekesegahagan*. When I first arrived at Frog Lake there were no buildings excepting my husband's house and warehouse — a shed and garden, added thereto, formed the whole establishment. These were built by my husband. Since then, in the course of three years that I was there, several buildings were put up, until, in fine, our little settlement became quite a village.

Mr. Quinn's, (the agent) house, and his storehouse, were erected since I arrived there. Mr. Quinn was the gentleman whose name has appeared so much in the public prints since the sad events of the second of April last. When I come to my experience during the last three months of my North-West life, I will give more fully the story of Mr. Quinn's fate. There were three reserves near us, the Indians upon which were

Frog Lake Settlement — Mr. Delaney's House Etc.

under my husband's control — In the next section of this chapter I will refer to these bands and give what I know about them.

The scenery around Frog Lake is surpassingly beautiful. We lived on Frog Creek, which runs from the Lake into the North Saskatchewan. In October last, Mr. Gowanlock, who shared the same fate as my husband, and whose kind and gentle wife was my companion through all the troubles and exposures of our captivity and escape, began to build a mill two miles from our place, on the waters of Frog Creek. He put up a saw mill and had all the timber ready to complete a grist mill, when he was cut short in his early life, and his wife was cast upon the mercy of Providence. They lived two miles from us. Many of those whom I knew were mill hands. Gilchrist who was killed, was an employee of Mr. Gowanlock.

Frog Lake is pretty large. I know that in one direction it is twelve miles long. In the centre of the lake is a large island, that is clothed in a garb of evergreen. The pine and spruce upon it are extra large, sound and plentiful. In fact it would be difficult to find a place where better timber for building and other purposes, could be cut. The place is gradually becoming developed, and when I consider all that has been done, in the way of improvement, since I first went there, I would not be surprised to learn, that in the near future, the principal parts of the country shall be under cultivation, that the clang of the mill shall be heard upon every stream, and that down the Saskatchewan may float the produce of a fresh, a virgin, a teeming soil, to supply the markets of the Old World, and to supplant the over-worked fields of the eastern countries.

Also since my arrival at the Frog Lake Reserve, the priest's house, the school house and church were built. Even there in the far west, away so to speak, from the atmosphere of civilization, beyond the confines of society, we have what Sir Alexander Selkirk mourned for so much, when alone on Juan Fernandez — *Religion.* Even there, the ministers of the Gospel, faithful to their duties, and mindful of the great command to "go forth and teach all nations," — leaving their homes and friends in the land of the east, seek out the children of those Indian tribes, and bring to them the lights of faith and instruction. Untiring in their exertions, indefatigable in their labors, they set a glorious example, and perform prodigies of good. The church was small, but neat, and although its ornaments are few, still I am sure that as fervent and as acceptable prayers went up, like incense, towards heaven, and blessings as choice, like dew, fell upon the humble worshippers, as ever the peal of the cathedral organ announced, or as ever decended [*sic*] upon the faithful beneath the gorgeous domes of the most splendid Basilicas. Memory still oftens [*sic*] summons up before me the scenes of silent, dusky, faithful children of the forest, kneeling in prayer, and with mingled feelings of awe, wonder, admiration and confidence, listening to the divine truths as explained in their own language, by the missionaries. But the picture becomes dark when I reflect upon the fate of the two good men whose sad story I have yet to tell. Most assuredly theirs was a *confession of blood* — and dying at their posts, faithful to their mission, relieving the soul of an expiring christian when the hand of death fell upon them. Theirs must have been a triumphal entry into heaven, to the kingdom of God! The great cross that the 90th Battalion placed over the united graves of the victims of the Frog Lake massacre, is a fitting emblem and a worthy monument; its base rests upon the soil that covers their union in the grave, but its summits [*sic*] points to where their souls are united above.

I will now take up the question of the Indians under my husband's control, and I will tell how they got along, improved, and were contented and happy. That will bring me to my last and all important chapter — the one which will contain the story so tragically mournful.

The Indians as They Are

It would not become me, perhaps, to comment upon the manner in which the country is governed, and the Indians instructed, for I am no politician. In fact I don't know one party from another except by name. But I cannot permit this occasion, the last I may ever have, to go past without saying plainly what I think and what I know about the north-west and its troubles.

The half-breeds, or whites or others may have real or imaginary grievances that they desire to see redressed. If they have, I know nothing about them; I never had anything to do with them and maybe I could not understand the nature of their claims, even if explained to me. But be that as it may — even if I did know aught I would not feel myself justified in writing down that which I could only have learned by hear say. But there is one thing I do know and most emphatically desire to express and have thoroughly understood and that is the fact, *the Indians have no grievances and no complaints to make.* Their treatment is of the best and most generous kind. The government spares no pains to attempt to make them adopt an agricultural life, to teach them to rely upon their own strength, to become independent people and good citizens. Of the Indians I can speak openly for I know them thoroughly. There may be, here and there, a bad man amongst them; but as a people they are submissive, kind, and, if only from curiosity, they are anxious to learn. My husband remarked that according as they advanced in their agricultural knowledge that they commenced to have a liking for it. And I noticed the same in the young squaws whom I undertook to instruct in household duties.

Many an English, Scotch [*sic*] or Irish farmer, when he comes poor to Canada and strives to take up a little farm for himself, if he had only one half the advantages that the government affords to the Indians, he would consider his fortune forever made. They need never want for food. Their rations are most regularly dealt out to them and they are paid to clear and cultivate their own land. They work for themselves and are, moreover, paid to do so — and should a crop fail they are certain of their food, anyway. I ask if a man could reasonably expect more? Is it not then unjust to lead these poor people into a trouble which can but injure them deeply! If half-breeds have grievances let them get them redressed if they chose [*sic*], but let them not mix up the Indians in their troubles. The Indians have nothing to complain of and as a race they are happy in their quite [*sic*] home of the wilderness and I consider it a great shame for evil-minded people, whether whites or half-breeds, to instill into their excitable heads the false idea that they are persecuted by the government. In speaking thus I refer to *our* Indians that is to say those under my late husband's control. But if all government agencies and reserves are like that at Frog Lake, I hesitate not to say, that the government is over good to the restless bands of the west.

I have no intention in my sketch to use any names — for if I mention one of my friends I should mention them all and that would be almost impossible. No more will I mention the names of any persons who might be implicated in the strange and dishonest acts that have taken place previous to, during and since the outbreak. Yet I feel it a duty to present a true picture of the situation of the Indian bands and of the two great powers that govern in the country and whose interests are the very opposite of each other.

These two governing parties are the Hudson Bay Company and the Dominion Government. There is not the slightest doubt, but their interests are directly opposed. The company has made its millions out of the fur trade and its present support is the same trade. The more the Indians hunt the more the Company can make. Now the Government desires to civilize them and to teach them to cultivate the soil. The more the Indian works on his farm the less the Company gets in the way of fur. Again, the more the Government supplies the Indians with rations the less the Company can sell to them.

Two buffalos are not given for a glass of whiskey — one-third highwines and two-thirds water — as when the Company had full sway. The fire-water is not permitted to be brought to them now. No longer have the Indians to pay the exorbitant prices for pork, flour, tea, &c., that the Company charged them. The Government has rendered it unnecessary for them to thus sacrifice their time and means. Did the Company ever try to civilize or christianize the Indians! Most certainly not. The more they became enlightened the less hold the Company would have upon them. Again, if it were not for the Government, the lights of the gospel would scarcely ever reach them. The more the Government civilizes them and developes [sic] the country, the less plentiful the the [sic] game becomes, and the less profit the Company can make. Therefore it is that I say, the interests of the Company and those of the Government are contradictory. The former wants no civilization, plenty of game, and Indians that will hunt all the year around. The latter require agriculture, the soil to be taken from the wild state, the rays of faith and instruction to penetrate the furthest recess of the land, and to have a race that can become worthy of the diginity [sic] of citizens in a civilized country. So much the worse for the Government if the Indians rebel and so much the worse for the Indians themselves; but so much the better for the Company's interests.

I have my own private opinions upon the causes of the rebellion but do not deem it well or proper to express them. There are others besides the half-breeds, and Big Bear and his men connected with the affair. There are many objects to be gained by such means and there is a "wheel within a wheel" in the North-West troubles.

As far as I can judge of the Indian character, they are not, at all, an agricultural people — nor for a few generations are they likely to become such. Their habits are formed, their lives are directed in a certain line — like a sapling you can bend at will and when grown into a tree you can no longer change its shape — so with them. From time immemorial they have ranged the woods and it is not in the present nor even the next generation that you can uproot that inclination. Take the negro from the south and place him amongst the ice-bergs of the arctic circle and strive to make him accustomed to the hunting of the seal or harpooning of the walruss; — or else bring down an Esquimaux [sic] and put him into a sugar-cane plantation of the topics [sic]. In fact, take a thorough going farmer from the old-country and attempt to accustom him to hunt moose and trap beaver. He may get expert at it; but give him a chance and he will soon fling away the traps and pick up the spade, lay down the rifle and take hold of the plough. So it is with the Indians — they may get a taste for farming, but they prefer to hunt. Even the best amongst them had to have a month every spring and another month every fall to hunt. And they would count the weeks and look as anxiously forward to those few days of freedom, of unbridled liberty, as a school-boy looks forward to his mid-summer holidays.

Yet, in spite of this hankering after the woods and the freedom of the chase, they are a people easily instructed, quick to learn, (when they like to do so), and very submissive and grateful. But they are very, very improvident. So long as they have enough for to-day, let to-morrow look out for itself. Even upon great festivals such as Christmas, when my husband would give them a double allowance of rations, they would come before our house, fire off their guns as a token of joy and thanks, and then proceed with their feast and never stop until they had the double allowance all eaten up and not a scrap left for the next day.

In my own sphere I was often quite amused with the young squaws. They used to do my house-work for me. I would do each special thing for them — from cleaning, scrubbing, washing, cooking to sewing, fancy work, &c. and they would rival each other in learning to follow me. They would feel as proud when they could perform some simple little work, as a child feels when he has learned his A.B.Cs. With time and care, good house-keepers could be made of many of them, and it is too bad to see so many clever, naturally gifted, bright creatures left in ignorance and misery. I think it was in Gray's Elegy that I read the line: "How many a flower is born to blush unseen, and waste its fragrance on the desert air."

When I look back over these three years, I feel a pang of more than sorrow. Ours was a happy home; I grew to like my surroundings, I became fond of my Indian protegees, and to crown all, in December last, Mrs. Gowanlock came to live near us. I felt that even though a letter from home should be delayed, that I would not feel as lonesome as before. My husband was generous to a fault. He was liked by all the bands; — our white neighbours were few, but they were splendid people, fast and true friends, and I might say since Mrs. Gowanlock arrived, I felt at home; I looked upon the place as my own, and the Indian children as my children; the same as my husband looked upon the men as his care, and they regarded him as a father. It was no longer to be a lonely life. It was to become a life of usefulness, joy, labor, peace and contentment. Such was the vision I had of the future, about the middle of last winter! But who knows what is in store for us! "There is a Providence that shapes our ends, rough-hew them as we will!"

I will here quote a few lines from deposition given at Regina: "When he, (my husband) first came up here, he had five bands to look after until a year ago, when the Chippewans were taken from his supervision and given to Mr. John Fitzpatrick. A little later, Mr. Fitzpatrick was transferred to another jurisdiction, and the Chippewans came again under my husband's care. He then had to look after the Chippewans, Oneepewhayaws, Mistoo-Kooceawsis and Puskeakeewins, and last year he had Big Bear's tribe. He was so engaged when the outbreak took place. All the Indians were very peaceably inclined and most friendly to us all. My husband was much respected, and really beloved by all under his care, and they seemed to be most attached to him. We were, therefore, greatly astonished at their action towards us, but after all it was only Big Bear's followers that showed their enmity towards us. These too, pretended to be most friendly, and have often told us, "that but for my husband they would have starved."

With this, I close my second chapter, and will now, in the third offer my readers a picture of the scenes from the first of April last until the close of the struggle.

THREE

The North-West Troubles

$\mathcal{T}$here are scenes that are hard to properly describe. There are parts of our lives that can never be reproduced or transmitted to others upon paper. As Father Abram J. Ryan, the Poet Priest of the South so beautifully tells us:

> *"But far on the deep there are billows,*
> *That never shall break on the beach;*
> *And I have heard Songs in the Silence,*
> *That never shall float into speech;*
> *And I have had dreams in the Valley,*
> Too lofty for language to reach. "

So with me and my story. However I may have succeeded so far in expressing what I desired to convey to the public, I feel confident that I am far from able to do justice to to [*sic*] this last chapter. The events crowd upon my mind in a sort of kaliedescope [*sic*] confusion and scarcely have the intention of giving expression to an idea, than a hundred others crop up to usurp its place in my mind. Although I will tell the story of the tragic events as clearly and as truthfully as is possible, still I know that years after this little sketch is printed, I will remember incidents that now escape my memory. One has not time, or inclination, when situated as I was, to take a cool survey of all that passes and commit to memory every word that might be said or remark that might be made. Notwithstanding the fear I have of leaving out any points of interest or importance, I still imagine that my simple narrative will prove sufficient to give an idea, imperfect though it may be, of all the dangers we passed through, the sufferings we underwent, and the hair-breadth escapes we had.

Up to the 30th of March, 1885, we had not the fiaintest [*sic*] idea that a rebellion existed, nor that half-breeds and Indians were in open revolt. On that day we received two letters, one from Captain Dickens, of Fort Pitt, and one from Mr. Rae, of Battleford. Mr. Dickens' letter was asking all the whites to go down to Fort Pitt for safety as we could not trust the Indians; and Mr. Rae's letter informed us of the "Duck Lake" battle and asking us to keep the Indians up there and not let them down to join Poundmaker. When we were informed of the great trouble that was taking place, Mr. and Mrs. Gowanlock were apprised of the fact and they came up to our place for safety. My husband had no fear for himself, but he had slight misgivings as to poor Mr. Quinn's situation. Mr. Quinn was the agent in that district and was a Sioux half-breed.

Johnny Pritchard, his interpreter, was a Cree half-breed. My husband decided at once not to go to Fort Pitt. It would be a shame for us, he thought, to run away and leave all the Government provisions, horses, &c., at the mercy of those who would certainly take and squander them, moreover he feared nothing from the Indians. His own band were perfectly friendly and good — and not ten days previous, Big Bear had given him a peace-pipe or *calumet*, and told him that he was beloved by all the band.

However, knowing the Indian character so well, and being aware that the more you seemed to confide in them the more you were liked by them, he and Mr. Quinn concluded to hold a council with the chiefs and inform them of the news from Duck Lake, impressing upon them the necessity of being good and of doing their work, and not minding those troublesome characters that were only bringing misery upon themselves.

Consequently, on the first of April, the council was held, but to their great astonishment and dismay, the Indians knew more than they did about the affair, and, in fact, the Indians knew all about the troubles, long before news ever reached us, at Frog Lake, of the outbreak. At the council were "Aimasis" (The King-bird), one of Big Bear's sons and "The Wandering Spirit." They said that Big Bear had a bad name, but now that he had a chance he would show himself to be the whiteman's friend. All day, the 1st of April, they talked and held council, and finally the Indians went home, after shaking hands with my husband. They then told him that the half-breeds intended to come our way to join Riel! that they also intended to steal our horses, but that we need not fear as they (the Indians) would protect us and make sure no horses would be taken and no harm would be done. They also told us to sleep quiet and contented as they would be up all night and would watch. Big Bear, himself, was away upon a hunt and only got to the camp that night, we did not see him until next morning. During that day, the Indians, without an exception, asked for potatoes and of course they got them. They said we did not need so much potatoes and they would be a treat for them as they meant to make a big feast that night and have a dance.

Now as to their statement about the half-breeds coming to take horses or anything else we did not know whether to believe them or not. Of course it would never do to pretend to disbelieve them. However, the shadow of a doubt hung over each of us. We knew that the Indians had a better knowledge of all that was taking place than we had, and since they knew so much about the troubles, it looked probable enough that they should know what movements the half-breeds were to make. And moreover, they seemed so friendly, so good-spirited and in fact so free from any appearance of being in bad humor, that it would require a very incredulous character not to put faith in their word. But on the other hand it seemed strange, that, if they knew so much about our danger, they never even hinted it to us until our men first spoke of it to them. However, be these things as they may, we felt secure and still something told us that all was not well: often to others as well as to Campbell's wizard,

> "The sun set of life, gives them mystical lore —
> And coming events cast their shadows before."

Thus we parted on the night of the first of April, and all retired to bed, to rest, to dream. Little did some amongst us [know] that it was to be their last sleep, their last rest upon imagine [*sic*] earth, and that before another sun would set, they would be "sleeping the sleep that knows no waking" — resting the great eternal rest from which they will not be disturbed until the trumpet summons the countless millions from the tomb. Secure as we felt ourselves, we did not dream of the deep treachery and wicked guile that prompted those men to deceive their victims. The soldier may lie down calmly to sleep before the day of battle, but I doubt if we could have reposed in such tranquility if the vision of the morrow's tragedy had flashed across our dreams. It is indeed better that we know not the hour, nor the place! And again, is it not well that we should ever be prepared, so that no matter how or when the angel of death may strike, we are ready to meet the inevitable and learn "the great Secret of Life and Death!"

At about half past-four on the morning of the second of April, before we were out of bed, Johnny Pritchard and Aimasis came to our house and informed my husband that the horses had been stolen by the half-breeds. This was the first moment that a real suspicion came upon our mind. Aimasis protested that he was so sorry. He said that no one, except himself and men, were to blame. He said that they danced nearly all night and when it got on towards morning that all fell asleep, and that the half-breeds must have been upon the watch, for it was then that they came and stole the horses. The two then left us and we got up. About an hour after, Aimises [*sic*] came back and told us not to mind the horses, as they would go and hunt for them and bring them back.

I since found out, that as the horses were only two miles away in the woods, they feared that my husband might go and find them himself and that their trick would be discovered. It is hard to say how far they intended, at that time, to go on with the bad work they had commenced.

In about half an hour some twenty Indians came to the house, Big Bear was not with them, nor had they on warpaint, and they asked for our guns, that is my husband's and Mr. Quinn's. They said they were short of firearms and that they wished to defend us against the half-breeds. No matter what our inclinations or misgivings might then be, we could not however refuse the arms. They seemed quite pleased and went away. An hour had scarcely elapsed when over thirty Indians painted in the most fantastic and hedious [*sic*] manner came in. Big Bear also came, but he wore no war-paint, He placed himself behind my husband's chair. We were all seated at the table taking our breakfast. The Indians told us to eat plenty as we would not be hurt. They also ate plenty themselves — some sitting, others standing, scattered here and there through the room, devouring as if they had fasted for a month.

Big Bear then remarked to my husband that there would likely be some shooting done, but for him not to fear, as the Indians considered him as one of themselves. Before we had our meal finished Big Bear went out. The others then asked us all to go up to the church with them. We consequently went, Mr. and Mrs. Gowanlock, Mr. Dill, Mr. Williscraft, my husband and myself.

When we arrived at the church the mass was nearly over. The Indians, on entering, made quite a noise and clatter. They would not remove their hats or headdresses, they would not shut the door, nor remain silent, in fact, they did anything they considered provoking and ugly. The good priest, the ill-fated Father Fafard, turned upon the altar and addressed them. He warned them of the danger of excitement and he also forbade them to do any harm. He told them to go quietly away to their camps and not disturb the happiness and peace of the community. They seemed to pay but little attention to what they heard, but continued the same tumult. Then Father Fafard took off his vestments and cut short the mass, the last that he was destined ever to say upon earth; the next sacrifice he would offer was to be his own life. He as little dreamed as did some of the others that before many hours their souls would be with God, and that their bodies would find a few days sepulchre beneath that same church, whose burnt ruins would soon fall upon their union in the clay.

The Indians told us that we must all go back to our place. We obeyed and the priests came also. When we reached the house the Indians asked for beef-cattle. My husband gave them two oxen. Some of the tribe went out to kill the cattle. After about an hour's delay and talk, the Indians told us to come to their camp so that we would all be together and that they could aid us the better against the half-breeds. We consequently started with them.

Up to this point, I might say, the Indians showed us no ill-will, but continually harped upon the same chord, that they desired to defend and to save us from the half-breeds. So far they got everything they asked for, and even to the last of the cattle, my husband refused nothing. We felt no dread of death at their hands, yet we knew that they were excited and we could not say what they might do if provoked. We now believed that the story of the half-breeds was to deceive us and throw us off our guard — and yet we did not suspect that they meditated the foul deeds that darkened the morning of the second of April, and that have left it a day unfortunately, but too memorable, in the annals of Frog Lake history.

When I now look back over the events, I feel that we all took a proper course, yet the most unfortunate one for those that are gone. We could have no idea of the murderous intentions on the part of the Indians. Some people living in our civilized country may remark, that it was strange we did not notice the peculiar conduct of the Indians. But those people know nothing either of the Indian character or habits. So far from their manner seeming strange, or extraordinary, I might say, that I have seen them dozens of times act more foolishly, ask more silly questions and want more rediculous [sic] things — even appear more excited. Only for the war-paint and what Big Bear had told us, we would have had our fears completely lulled by the seemingly open and friendly manner. I have heard it remarked that it is a wonder we did not leave before the second of April and go to Fort Pitt; I repeat, nothing at all appeared to us a sign of alarm, and even if we dreaded the tragic scenes, my husband would not have gone. His post was at home; he had no fear that the Indians would hurt him; he had always treated them well and they often acknowledged it; he was an employee of the Government and had a trust in hand; he would never have run away and left the Government horses, cattle, stores, provisions, goods, &c., to be divided and scattered amongst the bands, he even said so before the council day. Had he ran [*sic*] away and saved his life, by the act, I am certain he would be then blamed as a coward and one not trustworthy nor faithful to his position. I could not well pass over this part of our sad story without answering some of those comments made by people, who, neither through experience nor any other means could form an idea of the situation. It is easy for me to now sit down and write out, if I choose, what ought to have been done; it is just as easy for people safe in their own homes, far from the scene, to talk, comment and tell how they would have acted and what they would have done. But these people know no more about the situation or the Indians, than I know about the Hindoos, their mode of life, or their habits.

Before proceeding any further with my narrative — and I am now about to approach the grand and awful scene of the tragedy — I will attempt, as best I can, to describe the Indian war-paint — the costume, the head-dress and attitudes. I imagined once that all the stories that American novelists told us about the war-dance, — war-whoops, — war-paint, — war-hatchet or tomahawk, were but fiction drawn from some too lively imaginations. But I have seen them in reality, more fearful than they have ever been described by the pen of novelist or pencil of painter.

Firstly, the Indians adorn their heads with feathers, about six inches in length and of every imaginable color. These they buy from the Hudson Bay Company. Also it is from the Company they procure their paints. An Indian, of certain bands, would prefer to go without food than be deprived of the paint. Our Indians never painted, and in fact Big Bear's band use [*sic*] to laugh at the Chippewans for their quiet manners and strict observance of their religious duties. In fact these latter were very good people and often their conduct would put to the blush white people. They never would eat or even drink a cup of tea without first saying a grace, and then, if only by a word, thanking God for what they received. But those that used the paint managed to arrange their persons in the most abomonable [*sic*] and ghastly manner. With the feathers, they mix porcupine quills and knitt [*sic*] the whole into their hair — then daub their head with a species of white clay that is to be found in their country. They wear no clothing except what they call loin-cloth or breach-cloth, and when they go on the war-path, just as when they went to attack Fort Pitt, they are completely naked. Their bodies are painted a bright yellow, over the forehead a deep green, then streaks of yellow and black, blue and purple upon the eyelids and nose. The streaks are a deep crimson, dotted with black, blue, or green. In a word, they have every imaginable color. It is hard to form an idea of how hedious [*sic*] they appear when the red, blue, green and white feathers deck the head, the body a deep orange or bright yellow and the features tatooed in all fantastic forms. No circus clown could ever equal their ghostly decorations. When one sees, for the first time, these horrid creatures, wild, savage, mad, whether in that war-dance or to go on the war-path, it is sufficient to make the blood run cold, to chill the senses, to unnerve the stoutest arm and strike terror into the bravest heart.

Such was their appearance, each with a "greenary-yellowy" hue, that one assumes when under the electric light, when we all started with them for their camp. We were followed and surrounded by the Indians. The two priests, Mr. and Mrs. Gowanlock,

Mr. Gilchrist, Mr. Williscraft, Mr. Dill, Mr. Gouin, Mr. Quinn, my husband and myself formed the party of whites. My husband and I walked ahead. When we had got about one acre from the house we heard shots, which we thought were fired in the air. We paid little or no attention to them. I had my husband by the arm. We were thus linked when old Mr. Williscraft rushed past, bear-headed [*sic*]. I turned my head to see what was the cause of his excitement, when I saw Mr. Gowanlock fall. I was about to speak when I felt my husband's arm drop from mine — and he said, "I am shot too." Just then the priests rushed up and Father Fafard was saying something in French, which I could not catch. My husband staggered over about twenty feet from me and then back again and fell down beside me. I bent down and raised his head upon my lap. I think over forty shots must have been fired, but I could not tell what side the shot came from that hit my husband. I called Father Fafard and he came over. He knelt down and asked my husband if he could say the "confiteor." My husband said "yes" and then repeated the prayer from end to end. As he finished the prayer, the priest said: "my poor brother, I think you are safe with God," and as the words died upon his lips he received his death-wound and fell prostrate across my husband. I did not see who fired the shot. I only saw one shot fired; I thought it was for myself but it was for my husband and it finished him. In a couple of minutes an Indian, from the opposite side, ran up, caught me by the wrist and told me to go with him. I refused, but I saw another Indian shake his head at me and tell me to go on. He dragged me, by force away. I got one glance — the last — at my poor husband's body and I was taken off. After we had gone a piece I tried to look back — but the Indian gave me a few shakes pretty roughly and then dragged me through the creek up to my waist in water — then over a path full of thorns and briars and finally flung me down in his tent.

I will not now stay to describe my feelings or attempt to give in language, an idea of the million phantoms of dread and terror; memory seemed but too keen, and only too vividly could I behold the repetition of the scenes that had just passed before me. I stayed all day in the tent. I had the hope that some one would buy me off. Yet the hope was mingled with dispair [*sic*]. I thought if I could see Alec, one of our own Indians, that he would buy me, but I could not find out were [*sic*] he was. Towards evening I went to Johnny Pritchard's tent and asked him to buy me. He said he had been trying all day but could not succeed, however he expected to strike a bargain before night. He had only one horse and the Indians wanted two horses for me. As good luck would have it, he got Nolin — another half-breed — to give the second horse. It was all they had and yet they willingly parted with that *all*, to save me from inhuman treatment, and even worse than a hundred deaths. There was a slight relief in knowing that I was out of the power of the painted devil that held me, since my husband's death. But we were far from safe. Pritchard took me to his own tent, and placed me with his wife and family. There I felt that if there existed any chance of an escape at all I would be able to take advantage of it. I fully trusted to Pritchard's manliness and good character, and I was not deceived. He not only proved himself a sincere friend and a brave fellow, but he acted the part of a perfect gentleman, throughout, and stands, ever since, in my estimation the type of God's noblest creatures — A TRULY GOOD MAN.

For three weeks I was watched, as a cat would watch a mouse. All night long the

Indians kept prowling about the tent, coming in, going out, returning; they resembled, at times, a pack of wolves skulking around their prey, and, at times, they appeared to resemble a herd of demons as we see them represented in the most extravagant of frightful pictures. However, Pritchard spoke to them and their attentions became less annoying. They may have watched as closely as ever and I think they did, but they seldom came into my tent and when they did come in, it was only for a moment. I slept in a sitting position and whenever I would wake up, in a startled state from some fevered dream, I invariably saw, at the tent door, a human eye riveted upon me.

Imagine yourself seated in a quiet room at night, and every time you look at the door, which is slightly ajar, you catch the eye of a man fixed upon you, and try then to form an idea of my feelings. I heard that the human eye had power to subdue the most savage beast that roams the woods; if so, there must be a great power in the organ of vision; but I know of no object so awe-inspiring to look upon, as the naked eye concentrated upon your features. Had we but the same conception of that "all seeing eye," which we are told, continually watches us, we would doubtlessly be wise and good; for if it inspired us with a proportionate fear, we would possess what Solomon tells us in the first step to wisdom — "The fear of the Lord is the beginning of wisdom."

But I never could describe all the miseries I suffered during those few weeks. I was two months in captivity; and eight days afterwards we heard of Major-General Strange's arrival, I managed to escape. The morning of our escape seemed to have been especially marked out by providence for us. It was the first and only time the Indians were not upon the close watch. Up to that day, we used to march from sunrise to sunset, and all night long the Indians would dance. I cannot conceive how human beings could march all day, as they did, and then dance the wild, frantic dances that they kept up all night. Coming on grey dawn they would tier [*sic*] out and take some repose. Every morning they would tear down our tent to see if we were in it. But whether attracted by the arrival of the soldiers — by the news of General Strange's engagement — or whether they considered we did not meditate flight, I cannot say — but most certainly they neglected their guard that day.

Some of them came in as usual, but we were making tea, and they went off. As soon as the coast was clear we left our tea, and all, and we departed. Maybe they did not know which way we went, or perhaps they were too much engaged with their own immediate danger to make chase, but be that as it may, we escaped. It was our last night under the lynx-eyed watchers. We went about two miles in the woods, and there hid. So far I had no covering for my head, and but scant raiment for my body. The season was very cold in April and May, and many a time I felt numb, chill, and sick, but there was no remedy for it; only "grin and go through." In the last part of my captivity, I suffered from exposure to the sun. The squaws took all my hats, and I could not get anything to cover my head, except a blanket, and I would not dare to put one on, as I knew not the moment we might fall in with the scouts, and they might take me for a squaw. My shawl had become ribbons from tearing through the bush, and towards the end I was not able to get two rags of it to remain together. There is no possibility of giving an idea of our sufferings. The physical pains, exposures, dangers, colds, heats, sleepless nights, long marches, scant food, poor raiment, &c., would be bad enough, — but we must not loose [*sic*] sight of the mental anguish, that memory, only two [*sic*] faithful, would inflict upon us, and the terror that alternate hope and despair would compel us to undergo. I cannot say which was the worst. But when united, our sad lives seemed to have passed beneath the darkest cloud that could possibly hang over them.

When the Indians held their tea-dances or pow-wows in times of peace, the squaws and children joined in, and it was a very amusing sight to watch them. We often went three miles to look at a tea-dance, and I found it as attractive and interesting as a big circus would be to the children of a civilized place. But I had then no idea of the war-dance. They differ in every respect. No fire-arms are used at the tea-dance, and the guns and tomahawks and knives play the principal part in the war-dance. A huge fire throws its yellow, fitful light upon the grim spectre-like objects that bound, leap, yell and howl, bend and pass, aim their weapons, and using their tomahawks in a mimic warfare, a hideous pantomine, around and across the blaze. Their gesticulations summon up visions of murder, horror, scalps, bleeding and dangling at their belts, human hearts and heads fixed upon their spears; their yells resemble at times the long and distant howl of a pack of famished wolves, when on the track of some hapless deer; and again their cries, their forms, their actions, their very surroundings could be compared to nothing else than some infernal scene, wherein the demons are frantic with hell, inflamed passions. Each one might bear Milton's description in his "Paradise Lost," of Death:

> "The other shape
> If shape it might be called, that shape had none,
> Distinguishable, in member, joint or limb:
> *********
>
> black it stood as night.
> Fierce as ten Furies, terrible as hell,
> And shook a dreadful dart.—"

And the union of all such beings might also be described in the words of the same author:

> "The chief were those who from the pit of hell,
> Roaming to seek their prey on earth, durst fix
> Their seats, long after, next the seat of God,
> Their altars, by his altar; gods adored
> Among the nations round; and durst abide
> Jehovah thundering out of Sion, throned
> Between the cherubim; yea of ten placed
> Within his sanctuary itself their shrines,
> Abominations; and with cursed things
> His holy rites and solemn feasts profaned."

The scenes at the little church the morning of the second of April, — the massacre of God's anointed priests, the desecration of the temple, the robbery of the sacred vessels and ornaments, the burning of the edifice — are not those the deeds of beings not human, but infernal? Is the likeness too vivid or too true? But in the wild banquet of their triumph, while still holding the sacred vessels, they were checked as of old was Belshazzer. Those scenes shall never pass from my memory; with Freneau I can say:

"And long shall timorous fancy see,
The painted chief, the pointed spear;
And reason's self shall bow the knee,
To shadows and delusions here."

Now that I have passed once more over the trying scenes of the sad and eventful month of April, I will describe some of the dangers of our position, how we moved, camped, slept, and cooked. I will come to the transition from wild adventure to calm security, from the dangers of the wilderness to the safety of civilization. Once free from the toils of the Indians and back in the bosom of society, I will have but to describe our trip home, tell of the kindness received, and close this short sketch, bid "good-bye" to my kind and patient readers and return to that quiet life, which God in His mercy has reserved for me.

After our escape, we travelled all day long in the same bush, so that should the Indians discover us, we would seem to be still with them. We had nothing to eat but bread and water. We dare not make fire as we might be detected by the savages and then be subjected to a stricter *surveillance,* and maybe punished for our wanderings. Thus speaking of fire makes me think of the signals that the bands had, the beacons that flared from the heights at stated times and for certain purposes. Even before the outbreak, I remember of Indians coming to my husband and telling him that they were going on a hunt, and if such and such a thing took place, they would at a certain time and in a certain direction, make a fire. We often watched for the fires and at the stated time we would perceive the thin column of smoke ascend into the sky. For twenty and thirty miles around these fires can be seen. They are made in a very peculiar manner. The Indian digs a hole about a foot square and in that start the flame. He piles branches or fagots up on a cone fashion, like a bee-hive, and leaving a small hole in the top for the smoke to issue forth, he makes a draught space below on the four sides. If the wind is not strong, that tiny column of blue smoke will ascend to a height often of fifty or sixty feet. During the war times they make use of these fires as signals from band to band, and each fire has a conventional meaning. Like the *phares* that flashed the alarm from hill-top to hill-top or the tocsin that sang from belfry to belfry in the Basse Bretagne, in the days of the rising of the Vendee, so those beacons would communicate as swiftly the tidings that one band or tribe had to convey to another. Again, speaking of the danger of fire-making, I will give an example of what those Indians did with men of their own tribe.

A few of their men desired to go to Fort Pitt with their families, while the others objected. The couple of families escaped and reached the opposite side of a large lake. The Indians did not know which direction the fugitives had taken until noon the following day, when they saw their fire for dinner, across the lake. They started, half by one side and half by the other side of the lake, and came up so as to surround the fugitives. They took their horses, blankets, provisions, and camps, and set fire to the prairie on all sides so as to prevent the unhappy families from going or returning. When they thus treated their own people, what could white people expect at their hands?

The second day after our escape we travelled through a thicker bush and the men were kept busy cutting roads for us. We camped four times to make up for the day before, its fast and tramp. We made a cup of tea and a bannock each time. The third day we got into the open prairie, and about ten in the morning we lost our way. We were for over three hours in perplexity. We feared to advance too much as we might be getting farther from our proper track. About one o'clock the sun appeared and by means of it we regained our right course. At four we camped for the night. We found a pretty clump of poplars and there pitched our tents for a good repose. I had just commenced to make a bannock for our tea, when Pritchard ran in and told me that the police were outside and for me to go to them at once. I sincerely believe that it was at that moment we ran the greatest of all our risks. The police had taken us for a band of Indians, and were on the point of shooting at us when I came out and arrested the act. When they found who we were, they came in, placed their guns aside, and gave us some corned beef and "hard tack," a species of biscuit. These were luxuries to us, while our tea and bannock were a treat to them. We all had tea together, and then we went with them to the open prairie, where we travelled for about two hours. Next morning we moved into Fort Pitt. It was a glad sight to see the three steamboats, and both sailors, soldiers, and civilians gave me a grand reception.

Rescued!

It was upon Friday morning that we got into Fort Pitt, and we remained their [*sic*] until Sunday. On Friday night the military band came down two miles to play for us. It was quite an agreeable change from the "tom-tom" of the Indians. Next day we went to see the soldiers drill. If I am not mistaken there were over 500 men there. Sunday, we left per boat, for Battleford, and got in that night. We had a pleasant trip on the steamer "The Marquis." While at Fort Pitt we had cabins on board the very elegant vessel "North West." We remained three weeks at Battleford, expecting to be daily called upon as witnesses in some cases. We travelled overland from Battleford to Swift

Current, and thence by rail to Regina. At Moose Jaw, half way between Swift Current and Regina, we were greatly frightened. Such a number of people were collected to see and greet us, that we imagined it was Riel and his followers who had come to take us prisoners. Our fears were however, soon quelled. We remained four days at Regina; thence we came to Winnipeg. There we remained from Monday evening until Tuesday evening. Mostly all the people in the city came to see us, and I cannot commence to enumerate the valuable presents we received from the open- hearted citizens. We stoped [*sic*] with a Mrs. Bennett; her treatment to us, was like the care of a fond mother for her lost children.

We left on Thursday evening for Port Arthur, and thence we came by boat, to Owen Sound. A person not in trouble could not help but enjoy the glorious trip on the bosom of that immense inland sea. But, although we were overjoyed to be once more in safety, and drawing nearer our homes, yet memory was not sleeping, and we had too much to think off [*sic*] to permit our enjoying the trip as it could be enjoyed. From Owen Sound we proceeded to Parkdale by train. Parkdale is a lovely spot just outside of Toronto. I spent the afternoon there, and at nine o'clock that night left for home. I said good-bye to Mrs. Gowanlock; after all our sorrows, troubles, dangers, miseries, which we partook in union, we found it necessary to separate. And although we scarcely were half a year acquainted, it seemed as if we had been playmates in childhood, and companions throughout our whole lives. But, as we could not, for the present, continue our hand-in-hand journey, we separated merely physically speaking — for "time has not ages, nor space has not distance," to sever the recollections of our mutual trials.

I arrived home at 6 o'clock on Monday morning. What were my feelings as I stepped down from the hack, at that door, where three years before I stepped up into a carriage, accompanied by my husband! How different the scene of the bride leaving three years ago, and the widow returning today! Still, on the first occasion there were tears of regret at parting, and smiles of anticipated pleasure and happiness — on the second occasion there are tears of memory, and yet smiles of relief on my escape, and happiness in my safe return.

My story draws to a close "Like a tale that is told," it possesses, perhaps, no longer any interest for my readers. Yet, before dropping the veil upon the past, and returning to that life, out of which I had been forced by adverse circumstances. Before saying good-bye to the public forever, I feel that I have a few concluding remarks which I should make, and which I will now offer to my readers as an *adieu!*

CONCLUSION

St. THOS. A. KEMPIS, in his beautiful " Imitation of Christ," asks: "who is it that has all which he wishes for? Not I, not you, nor any man upon earth." Although, we often are disappointed in our expectations of happiness, and fail to attain all we desire, yet we have much to be thankful for. I have passed through more than I ever expected I would be able to bear; and still I feel most grateful, and I would not close this short sketch, without addressing a few words to those who are objects of my gratitude.

Firstly, to my readers, I will say that all I have told you, in these few passages, is the simple truth; nothing added thereto, nothing taken therefrom. You have toiled through them despite the poverty of composition and the want of literary style upon them; and now that the story is told, I thank you for your patience with me, and I trust that you may have enjoyed a few moments of pleasure at least, while engaged in reading.

Secondly, let me say a word to my friends of the North-West, and to those of Canada, I cannot name anyone in particular, as those whose kindness was great, yet whose names were accidently omitted, would feel perhaps, that I slighted their favors. Believe me, one and all, that (in the words of a great orator of the last century), "my memory shall have mouldered when it ceases to recall your goodness and kindness, my tongue shall forever be silent, when it ceases to repeat your expressions of sympathy, and my heart shall have ceased to beat when it throbs no longer for your happiness."

The troubles of the North-West have proven that there is no land, however, happy, prosperous or tranquil it may be, that is totally free from the dangers of internal revolts, — it has likewise proven that our country possesses the means, the strength, the energy and stamina, to crush the hydra of disunion or rebellion, no matter where it may appear. For like the upas tree, if it is permitted to take root and grow, its proportions would soon become alarming, while its poisonous influence would pollute the atmosphere with misery, ruin, rapine and death.

The rebellion is now a thing of the past. It is now a page in Canadian history. When a few generations shall come and go; our sad story of the "Frog Lake Massacre," may be totally forgotten, and the actors therein consigned to oblivion; but, these few papers, should they by any chance, survive the hand of time, will tell to the children of the future Canada, what those of your day experienced and suffered; and when those who are yet to be, learn the extent of the troubles undergone, and the sacrifices made by those of the present, to set them examples worthy of imitation, and models fit for their practice, to build up for them a great and solid nation, they may perhaps reflect with pride upon the history of their country, its struggles, dangers, tempests and calms. In those days, I trust and pray that Canada may be the realization of that glowing picture of a grand nation, drawn by a Canadian poet:—

> *"The Northern arch, whose grand proportions,*
> *Spans the sky from sea to sea,*
> *From Atlantic to Pacific—*
> *Home of unborn millions free!"*

The heartfelt sympathy of the country has been expressed in many forms, and ever with deep effect, and has twined a garland to drop upon the graves of those who sleep to-night away in the wilds of the North-West. Permit me to add one flower to that chaplet. You who are mothers, and know the value of your dutiful sons, while living, and have felt the greatness of their loss, when dead; you, who are sisters, and have known a brother's affection, the recollection of which draws you at times to his last resting place, to decorate that home of the dead with a forget-me-not; you, above all, who have experienced the love and devotion of a husband, and have mourned over that flower which has forever faded in death — you will not hesitate in joining with me, as I express, though feebly, my regret, and bring my sincerest of tributes to place upon the lonely grave by the Saskatchewan. Its united waters will sing their *requiem* while I say with Whittier:

> *"Green be the turf above thee,*
> *Friend of my better days;*
> *None knew thee but to love thee,*
> *None named thee but to praise!"*

End

THE SASKATCHEWAN STREAM

$\mathcal{M}$r. Delaney while in Ontario on a visit from the North-West, in the year 1882, for the purpose of taking back a bride, gave vent to the following beautiful words:

I long to return to the far distant West,
Where the sun on the prairies sinks cloudless to rest,
Where the fair moon is brightest and stars twinkling peep;
And the flowers of the wood soft folded in sleep.

Oh, the West with its glories, I ne'er can forget,
The fair lands I found there, the friends I there met,
And memory brings back like a fond cherished dream;
The days I have spent by Saskatchewan stream.

By dark Battle river, in fancy I stray,
And gaze o'er the blue Eagle Hills far away,
And hark to the bugle notes borne o'er the plain,
The echoing hills giving back the refrain.

Ah, once more I'll go to my beautiful West,
Where nature is loveliest, fairest and best:
And lonely and long do the days to me seem,
Since I wandered away from Saskatchewan stream.

Ontario, home of my boyhood farewell,
I leave thy dear land in a fairer to dwell,
Though fondly I love thee, I only can rest,
'Mid the flower strewn prairie I found in the West

And as by the wide rolling river I stray,
Till death comes at night like the close of the day,
The moon from the bright starry heavens shall gleam
On my home by the banks of Saskatchewan stream.